Collaborative
School
Reviews

Collaborative
School
Reviews

How to Shape Schools From the Inside

Beverley Freedman
Raffaella Di Cecco

A JOINT PUBLICATION

CORWIN
A SAGE Company

FOR INFORMATION:

Corwin

A SAGE Company

2455 Teller Road

Thousand Oaks, California 91320

(800) 233-9936

www.corwin.com

SAGE Publications Ltd.

1 Oliver's Yard

55 City Road

London, EC1Y 1SP

United Kingdom

SAGE Publications India Pvt. Ltd.

B 1/I 1 Mohan Cooperative Industrial Area

Mathura Road, New Delhi 110 044

India

SAGE Publications Asia-Pacific Pte. Ltd.

3 Church Street

#10–04 Samsung Hub

Singapore 049483

Printed in the United States of America.

A catalog record of this book is available from the Library of Congress.

ISBN 9781452242958

Acquisitions Editor: Arnis Burvikovs

Associate Editor: Desirée Bartlett

Editorial Assistant: Mayan White

Production Editor: Amy Schroller

Copy Editor: Gretchen Treadwell

Typesetter: Hurix Systems Pvt. Ltd

Proofreader: Victoria Reed-Castros

Indexer: Maria Sosnowski

Cover Designer: Candice Harman

Permissions Editor: Jennifer Barron

This book is printed on acid-free paper.

SFI label applies to text stock

13 14 15 16 17 10 9 8 7 6 5 4 3 2 1

Contents

For further information and additional resources, please visit the website associated with this book at www.collaborativeschoolreviews.com.

Acknowledgments

In addition to our own combined experience, many colleagues have contributed to the making of this resource, notably Marjatta Longston and Lisa Millar who are instructional leaders at a system and provincial level in their own right. We also have quotes from practicing system leaders Mike Borgfjiord and Lesleigh Dye. We have learned immeasurably from the Toronto District School Board's School Effectiveness Team of Kathy Cowan, Annie Appleby, Linda Curtis, and Leslie Banner, Bev's partners on many reviews. Thanks to Susan Schwartz, Karen Grose, Susan Murray, Nina Bascia, Jennifer Adams, Joan Powell, Mark Smiley, Dafna Ross, Roula Anastasakos, Linda Massie, and especially the Ontario Principals' Council for their ongoing support and feedback. Thanks to Jason Canavan for his assistance creating graphics. A special thanks to Barbara Bodkin and Angela Piscitelli for their friendship, support, and encouragement. Last, a debt of gratitude to our husbands, Lorenzo and Jon, and our families for their patience.

The resource is influenced by the works of Barber, Bernhardt, Crevola, DuFour, Elmore, Harris, Hattie, and Marzano, among others. Coming from Ontario, we owe a debt of gratitude to Michael Fullan, Ken Leithwood, Ben Levin, Avis Glaze, Lyn Sharratt, Mary Jean Gallagher, and the governments that have enabled excellence in Ontario schools. They have shaped education reform across that province which the Organisation for Economic Co-operation and Development (OECD) has acknowledged as an innovative and successful jurisdiction. For further information and additional resources, please visit the website associated with this book (www.collaborativeschool reviews.com).

Publisher's Acknowledgments

Corwin would like to thank the following individuals for their editorial insight and guidance:

Dr. Peter DeWitt, Elementary School Principal/Corwin Author
Averill Park Central School District
Poestenkill, NY

Mary Johnstone, Director
AdvancED Alaska
Anchorage, AK

Tom Lindsay, Assistant Superintendent
Mannheim School District 83
Franklin Park, IL

Natalie Marston, Principal
Central Special School
Edgewater, MD

Dr. Sara E. Spruce, Professor of Education
Olivet Nazarene University
Bourbonnais, IL

Dr. Gayle Wahlin
Retired Assistant Superintendent, Currently Educational Consultant
DuPage Regional Office of Education
Wheaton, IL

About the Authors

Beverley (Bev) Freedman, EdD, is an educational consultant, involved in numerous district and provincial reviews, strategic planning, and system improvement. Currently she is supporting school districts in their implementation of reviews in Ontario and has led several provincial leadership and special education reviews. She is a trainer in several types of classroom observations. She presents on issues of principal instructional leadership, equity and inclusive education and evidence-informed decision making, and works with several independent schools on school improvement planning. In any one year, as an instructional leadership trainer, she visits hundreds of classrooms in a variety of schools and districts including districts in Manitoba, Nova Scotia, New Brunswick, and Newfoundland and outside Canada including Chile.

Bev has presented at numerous provincial, national, and international research conferences including the American Education Research Association, Congress for Humanities and Social Science, the International Congress for School Effectiveness and Improvement, and the International Principals' Congress. She coordinates professional learning for Canada's Outstanding Principals in collaboration with the Learning Partnership. She was superintendent of programs for the Durham District School Board and the former executive officer for the Ontario Ministry of Education's Literacy and Numeracy Secretariat (LNS). She worked as the leadership coordinator for the Faculty of Education, York University and remains affiliated with the Ontario Institute for Studies in Education, University of Toronto, and the University of Ontario's Institute of Technology. She was on the executive of Ontario's Provincial Superintendents' Organization (OPSOA), and in 2001, was named Ontario's Distinguished Leader by OPSOA. Her doctoral thesis won the Doctoral Dissertation Award from Phi Delta Kappa University of Toronto (PDK-UT) Chapter and she won the Larry Frase award from Curriculum Management Services Inc. (CMSi) in 2007. She is on the boards of Scientists in School, Licensed to Learn, and Teacher Mentor's Abroad.

Raffaella (Raf) DiCecco, CMC, is an authority on managing complex policy and program reform within a government environment at the provincial, federal, and local level. She has held senior positions at both the federal and provincial level in a variety of policy fields, in positions ranging from direct program delivery to policy development and program design. She has an expert understanding of educational, social, and labor market issues, policies, and delivery mechanisms. As regional director of education, she provided oversight for fifty-two school districts and as executive director of the Ontario Royal Commission on Learning (www.edu.gov.on.ca/eng/general/abcs/rcom/main.html), she directed the first review of Ontario's elementary and secondary education system in twenty-five years. The Commission's report *For the Love of Learning,* tabled in 1995, has established the foundation for Ontario's current reform agenda.

Raf has extensive experience in strategic planning and organizational development as both a senior executive and an organizational development professional. Her consulting practice focuses on change management and specifically the educational and employment sectors. Her clients include the public sector, the broader public sector, as well as the not-for-profit and the private sector. She has led major program reviews and evaluations within the education and employment sectors, has extensive experience as a facilitator building coalitions, and is well regarded as a coach and mentor. Her work has given her a unique understanding of the relationships between educational interests and the range of players and stakeholders; she brings this understanding to this resource.

Raf is a Certified Management Consultant (CMC) through the Canadian Association of Management Consultants and a member of the Canadian Evaluation Society.

Introduction

Investment in education is not only about money, it's also an investment in people and an investment in the future.

(Organisation for Economic Co-operation and Development [OECD], 2011)

IMPROVING SCHOOLS MATTER

Globally there is an increasing demand for better schools and improved outcomes for all students. The sense of urgency is aggravated by concerns about the future, the current state of internationally linked economies, and the need to ensure that our children will be well positioned in the global market place to become successful and independent. Governments see education as a key strategy and have adopted accountability for educational results as a cornerstone of their political agendas. Improvement is demanded; standards are being enforced. The requirement for evidence about improved student achievement is a fact of life and the pressure on school systems to deliver better results grows exponentially as concerns about the economy mount. This means that schools and school systems must move from analysis to action using feedback based on evidence of student achievement improvements.

A search in Google for "school improvement" yields 135 million hits. Clearly, people and experts are saying a lot about this topic. Not surprisingly, there is controversy and contradiction. At the core of this contradiction is the perceived tension between the aspiration to be collaborative instructional leaders and the growing demands for greater accountability. The first is based on taking time and building relationships and capacity as required while the need to immediately deliver improved results drives the second. How does one integrate collegiality and accountability? How does one resolve this seeming disconnect? How does one know if the intended directions and strategies are working? How does one provide assurance that improvement is happening when results seem to be lagging? Traditionally, external monitoring mechanisms for schools and school systems have been formal, hierarchical, and very high-stakes. Examples of these are national and state or provincial exams, school inspections, and school or district audits. While these can be effective external pressures to drive accountability and change, the fact is that these are processes done or perceived to be done *to* schools and not *with* schools. It is not a surprise that the primary reaction is often one of compliance. When the source of the external pressure is removed the tendency is to maintain the status quo and more familiar and often less productive ways of conducting work.

As former superintendents, school inspectors, auditors, and senior administrators, we appreciate how nerve-racking it can be to have a team of external "experts" descend on your school or school system and apply externally created standards as a lens to assess what you are doing. Many of these efforts are based on a deficit model, which then frames the findings in terms of shortcomings. We have been on the receiving and delivery end of such high-stakes accountability efforts and understand how disheartening and disabling this can be for those who really want to make changes. The lack of involvement and introspective examination of "what we do," gathering evidence about how well this works, and exploring "how we might do it better" becomes a real barrier to effective conversations about change and how to go about it.

WHY A RESOURCE ON SCHOOL REVIEWS

The need for a resource on school reviews is something that both of us have been thinking about as we have been conducting different types of reviews within educational systems. In this book, we demonstrate how our construct of *collaborative school reviews* can be used to deal with this apparent disconnect, and advocate the application of a collegial approach within existing structures and budgets while advancing the effective reshaping of schools with a heightened sense of immediacy. Our approach reshapes from the inside out and blends two seemingly contradictory strategies. Recognizing the sense of urgency, our model incorporates the traditional use of data-driven evidence with a logic model that focuses on the connection between inputs (teaching strategies) and results (student achievement data). This plus the overlay of collaboration and a change management model distinguishes our concept of collaborative school reviews from other models of school reviews currently in practice. We weave three outcomes throughout this resource: (1) increased and intentional coherence across classrooms and schools, (2) positive accountability, and (3) targeted capacity building linked to student achievement. Our aim is to demonstrate how to decrease the variability among and between schools and enhance coherency and intentionality to realize increased student results.

One of the things we hope this book will provoke is dialogue focused on the key drivers of change leading to collaborative improvement, especially at a time of systemic reform such as the implementation of the Common Core State Standards (CCSS) or the drive to dramatically improve student achievement on national and international assessments. We want to foster conversations based on the collective responsibility and involvement required for improving instruction in schools and school systems. This innovative process can be applied at a district and a school level depending on your role and need. The aim is ease of implementation and sustainability of changes.

WHAT MAKES THIS APPROACH DIFFERENT?

Our model differs from other types of school reviews in terms of the following characteristics:

- The reviews are designed as change management strategies.
- The focus is building collaborative relationships among staff.
- The aim is to engage staff in building shared understanding, accountability, and commitment to improving learning to impact achievement.
- Capacity building is an embedded component of the process.
- A work plan for moving forward is a requirement.

In our model, the school selects the areas of focus and has more control on how the design and planning of the reviews emerge. This design requires collaboration between the school and district. Collaboration and attention to evidence support innovation and change. Our starting point is collaborative school reviews that are designed and implemented in partnership rather than reviews imposed on schools.

We build our proposed collaborative school review process within a strategic change management framework that is grounded on accountability and responsibility.

- Schools reflect on the impact of their teaching strategies on student learning.
- Schools select the areas of learning where they want feedback, but always within the district's predefined improvement priorities and focus.

- School staff work with district staff to mold the process, but within a common districtwide review framework.
- School staff are part of the analysis and the solution, but within a shared data management environment.
- School staff build the collaborative school review improvement plan, but within the districtwide improvement agenda.
- School staff take responsibility for implementing changes, but within a prescribed accountability framework.

The use of a strategic change management framework based on continuous improvement ensures that the school's analysis is robust and informed so that selection of the areas for feedback is focused and germane to improved student outcomes.

- As the intent is to shape school reform from the inside out, a collective learning process, for the schools and the district based on continuous improvement, is integral to the design of each review.
- Capacity building is a component of the process: it is a non-negotiable of the review process.
- Staff engagement is a key driver: it is used to build the collective sense of purpose and urgency required to make significant, timely, and sustained changes.

We regard collaborative school reviews not as isolated unique incidents, but rather as components of the larger system's improvement agenda. Too often, schools view themselves as fiefdoms and not part of a coherent, interdependent, and focused school system. Too often, districts overwhelm schools with a myriad of demands and initiatives. To be sustainable and flourish, initiatives for school improvement need to be focused and aligned as well as contextualized and supported by the larger system. We weave this into the resource. Schools working independently as well as districts working to coordinate larger system improvement can benefit.

Our Lens Is the School

If you are in the midst of implementing change initiatives and want to understand if you are on track, or if you have implemented and you want to assess impact, collaborative school reviews grounded in shared accountability are a very powerful resource. We firmly believe that the expertise to improve the work that educators do resides within each school and school system: the real solutions and answers lie with staff. The trick is to extract this expertise and harness it into a planned and systematic improvement process engendering a collegial approach where learning is for everyone and everyone contributes to the development of effective practices. This is what we model.

THIS IS A HOW-TO RESOURCE

Collaborative school reviews are a path to improvement. This book provides a resource on how to go about designing, planning, implementing, and monitoring the effectiveness of school reviews. We combine research with practice. In Chapter 1, we explore big questions, and set the stage by introducing our strategic change management framework as the organizer for collaborative school reviews. Chapter 2 focuses on the design of the collaborative school review process. Chapters 3 and 4 investigate planning at the district and school levels, respectively. Chapter 5 provides three examples for the rollout of reviews and Chapter 6 examines how to unpack findings at the local and district level including analysis, feedback, and action planning through monitoring to ensure follow through. If you are reading this through the school lens you may want to bypass the district components and look at only the school-based components. In Chapter 7, we draw our conclusions. Each chapter includes tools, examples, and areas for discussion as well as a summary. Throughout we talk about what the district needs to tightly hold to ensure a systemic benefit and what can be loosely held in the purview of the schools under review.

How It Can Help You

We know improving the quality of schools is important to you. This resource provides a range of choices based on your unique requirements. We are not imposing standards that are external to your district or school.

- We examine how the improvement and change process is influenced by your context and culture, and discuss how these might be factored into your design.
- The embedded practical tools and forms offer choices and models for consideration as you apply the process to your own setting.
- Questions are posed as "Reader Reflections." You can use these as an inquiry focus for your own learning teams.
- The strategic lens provides a framework and organizer for the review process by focusing on the four key components of management: (1) design, (2) planning, (3) implementation, and (4) monitoring and evaluation.
- To make the process more accessible for you—the reader—we present our information through a case study, Lone Birch School District.

The district, schools, and educators described are loosely based on an amalgam of real schools that have been part of actual school review processes that we have conducted. We use this case study format to blend theory and best practice within the lens of a real-world situation. We deal with those issues that are representative of both larger and smaller school boards as well as urban, rural, and remote districts. We demonstrate how to gather and analyze data from reviews to identify trends, patterns, and outliers to build a data tapestry.

● Additionally, we show how this can be used at the district level to inform future reviews and to establish benchmarks for improvement.

This resource can be used effectively by district teams, while stand-alone schools, including independent or private schools, will also find the model applicable. In summary, our model differs from other models both in its intentionality and design. It is the product of our collective eighty years experience.

For further information and additional resources, please visit the website associated with this book at www.collaborativeschoolreviews.com.

1 Setting the Stage

This chapter introduces our concept of *collaborative school reviews* as opportunities for transformational school- and district-based change, our strategic lens as a framework for shaping and organizing the process, and then our case study as a practical illustration to apply the process. We blend theory with practices known to be effective to improve teaching and learning in schools and classrooms with a goal of raising standards and narrowing achievement gaps.

COLLABORATIVE SCHOOLS REVIEWS

A Path for Improvement

What Is a School Review?

A school review is a methodical assessment of the connection between the processes and activities that the school and district believe ought to contribute to student achievement and the student achievement evidential data. Typically, the review is conducted by a team of educators examining student achievement data, observing processes and activities, and providing findings and recommendations. Unlike audits and inspections, school review teams are drawn from the school district but its members are external to the school being reviewed. While audits and inspections are summative, school reviews are formative. They are part of the learning process for improvement. Inspections and audits follow prescribed structures and standards and can examine a wide range of information from governance, facilities, staffing, policies, and budgets, in addition to teaching and learning. Recommendations stemming from inspections and audits may or may not be mandated. School reviews, on the other hand, narrow the reviewing lens by specifically focusing on teaching and learning, and emphasizing a few key areas drawn from the school's data that are known to be directly linked to improved learning and student achievement.

What Distinguishes Collaborative School Reviews From Other Reviews?

Time and resources are limited commodities. External audits and reviews can be costly. We thus emphasize the collegial approach, the effective use of time and resources, and the need to develop shared understanding and practices within a structured format. Collaborative school reviews are a partnership between the district and school aimed at improving teaching and learning at the school and classroom level. For us, the essential considerations include the following:

- *Both districts and schools matter.* Collaborative school reviews are a districtwide effort, but the process needs to be contextualized to meet individual district and school needs and realities.
- *Improved learning and teaching practice are the focus.* Collaborative school reviews use the school's own improvement plan to explore which effective practices are being implemented from the improvement plan and which are not. The school gathers evidence of instructional and curricular practices that are research-informed and designed to increase student learning and achievement. For instance, what evidence is there of balanced literacy or the implementation of practices aligned to the Common Core State Standards (CCSS)?
- *Collaborative school reviews are a cost-effective way of continuous improvement and should be seen as part of the overall leadership and management role.* There is no need to hire external staff or contract out. Internal roles can be redesigned, time designated, and funding reallocated from other less impactful priorities and strategies. This repositioning of roles may require some initial investment in capacity building but this would in the long run yield significant benefits for the students and for the system. The process is grounded on building the skills and capacity of staff at a school and system level. It's all about learning.
- *Schools are the unit of change.* The school collaboratively selects the areas it wants to highlight and focuses on improved school learning aligned to the district's priorities or goals. These initial selections include areas for reinforcement, where the school staff perceives gains are being made but wants to continue to improve, and areas where staff may still be at the awareness level and implementation varies widely and requires critical feedback to move

the school further along the continuum of change, for instance, implementing strategies such as an increased use of informational text, analyzing texts, or the effective use of technology. The school gathers and selects the evidence creating a data portrait to support the areas of focus and areas for feedback to highlight during the review process. This is an opportunity for school faculties to collaborate in gathering and presenting schoolwide evidence as indicators of success for their areas of focus. Because the staff determines the areas of focus, buy-in occurs and it is easier to engage school staff in the review process and develop their collective ownership for proposed improvement strategies.

● *The link to district priorities is a critical requirement to ensure connectivity and coherence with district directions.* By ensuring this as a component in preparation for the review, the school staff becomes better informed about and more likely to engage with district goals and priorities. This reduces the differences among and between schools in terms of implementing effective practice that impact student learning; it develops greater understanding of how each unique school fits within the overall context of the broader system.

● *All aspects of classrooms count.* The external review team visits every instructional space during their onsite visit to determine coherency and intentionality across classrooms with regard to the areas of focus designated by the school. Research documents the persistence of detrimental variations in teacher practice even among teachers in the same building and even when the school implemented comprehensive and prescriptive whole-school reforms (Fullan, 2011; Hattie, 2012). Feedback on the degree of alignment of practice across classrooms can thus support effective learning.

● *Reviews are formative.* The goal is *assessment for learning.* Data are used to inform the school's improvement plan and improvement implementation process. All participants need to be able to take the feedback to inform practice. Think of the outcome of these reviews as descriptive feedback.

● *Collaborative school reviews use a change management framework to build a culture of continuous improvement and growth.* The assumption is that we are along a continuum of improvement. All schools are included in an ongoing cycle of reviews. The reports from the collaborative school reviews focus on areas of strength and areas for improvement at a school and district level. They can be layered for analysis to move the schools and districts along the continuum of good to great.

● *Collaborative school reviews create a data tapestry.* Evidence regarding learning and student success is gathered and monitored from a variety of data sources including onsite classroom visits. In addition to constructing this data tapestry, the collaborative school review model requires that goals and targets for improvement be directly linked to the district's and the data collection ensures that improvement can be tracked. It provides an opportunity to build data literacy and the ability to effectively use data to enhance teaching practice and ultimately student learning.

● *School improvement is a shared process.* Staff are involved in developing findings and actively participate in the development of the go-forward agenda. The findings are unpacked at the school level, with a key focus on the right findings and identifying appropriate high-yield strategies. External resources and expertise can enrich the findings and increase the viability of the actions for moving forward. Collaborative school reviews provide an opportunity for the school to access external expertise and supports.

● *Learning is a collective process both at the school and district level.* The review team is external to the school, but drawn from the local district. The external review team members have a better understanding of the district's unique culture and context and bring added expertise and experience but not added cost. Internally, the key is openness to the examination of one's teaching practice and participation in the development of improvement strategies. This happens best when teachers see the review as an opportunity to learn and grow collectively and not as a punitive measure. By linking best practices across the district, teachers can better learn from one another both within and beyond their specific school community. This means that capacity building becomes an element that has to be strictly guided and driven by need rather than want. Thus this becomes an opportunity to better focus capacity-building efforts to more effectively meet both district priorities and school needs.

● *Effective collaborative school reviews are respectful of educators' professionalism, recognizing that context and leadership are significant considerations.* We demonstrate how the jurisdictions, the drivers, and the expectations and vision for the school leadership role (principal, head teacher) can be carefully factored in when designing and implementing collaborative school reviews. They support the development of their skills as change leaders.

● *Collaborative school reviews are not a one-size-fits-all model.* The concepts we propose can be customized to apply across systems and an existing range of practices.

ACHIEVING EXCELLENCE

A Strategic Lens to Conceptualize Collaborative School Reviews

A key requirement for school improvement is for the overall organization to provide the wrap-around supports a school needs to achieve excellence. The collaborative school review model requires a direct tie between the school review process and the system's broader effectiveness effort such as implementing 21st-century learning or Common Core State Standards (CCSS). This ensures that the changes made at the school level are coherent and in sync with the system direction. Without this tie, change is likely to be sporadic and individualized and consequently less likely to be sustainable.

We overlay our vision for collaborative school reviews with a four-quadrant strategic framework and anchor the review process within a continuous improvement model. The four quadrants comprise the four key components of an effective strategic management process: (1) policy and program design, (2) planning, (3) implementation and monitoring, (4) assessment and adjustment. These quadrants are both sequential and interconnected with actions in one quadrant depending on and being informed by actions and data in the others (see Figure 1.1).

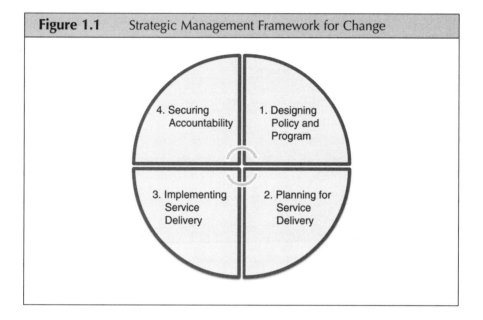

Figure 1.1   Strategic Management Framework for Change

The four-quadrant lens provides the framework to ensure that collaborative school reviews become a more thoughtful and analytical process; it also allows data to drive the organization's decisions about its directions, strategies, adjustments to policy and programs, and delivery strategies and mechanisms. This includes data about external drivers and best practices as well as internal evidence of how the organization functions and how well it is achieving its mandate and goals.

We examine the collaborative school review process, key tasks, and activities within the context and prerogatives of each of these four quadrants. These provide a disciplined approach and a broader strategic perspective for the collaborative school review. Each element is examined, contextualized, and addressed in a logical, feasible, and systematic manner to strategically focus the collaborative school review on essential improvement. Figure 1.2 demonstrates how this lens will apply to the school review process.

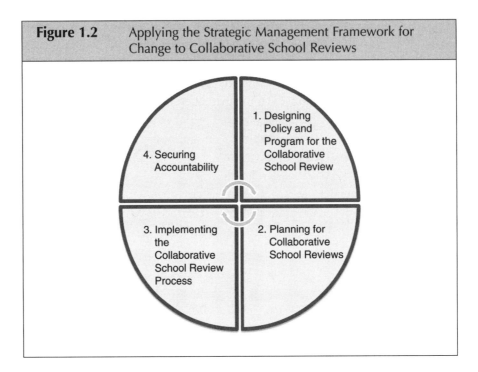

Figure 1.2 Applying the Strategic Management Framework for Change to Collaborative School Reviews

Figure 1.3 provides a discussion of each quadrant—what it involves and how we propose to apply it to the collaborative school review process.

As educators, we often spend our time in the day-to-day implementation issues—what we call Quadrant 3, or the delivery quadrant—failing to realize the importance of doing work in the other quadrants to ensure we have the proper direction, structure, and resourcing in place to achieve our goals. This attention is essential to ensure that we have focused on the right things and have drawn our conclusions based on evidence. What we are looking for is a proactive and rational way to proceed that is widely understood and supported within the district and not just a reactive, individually led, and isolated approach to change. The goal is to achieve greater intentionality and coherency in developing effective collaborative practice to support academic achievement and close gaps both within an individual school and across a system of schools. This is what is required to embed and sustain improvement.

Collaborative School Reviews as Opportunities for Transformational Change

Is the intended really happening in schools and classrooms? We recognize that there are a variety of obstacles that challenge the implementation of systemic change: wide variability in quality across classrooms and schools, the punitive use of accountability measures, and fragmented and nonaligned professional development. Using collaborative school reviews is a strategic

Figure 1.3   The Four-Quadrant Approach

- **Quadrant 1** anchors the organization through an emphasis on the ties to organizational vision, mission, and direction—and subsequently to policy formulation, strategy development, and program design. It calls for the organization to systematically pause and think strategically about what it might achieve and to strategize how it will do that. It puts an emphasis on the use of data garnered through the other quadrants to ground it in the here and now so that it can look at ways to develop and improve. This is where the organization establishes its mission, sets a vision and goals, develops its strategy, and determines its course of action.

- **Quadrant 2** focuses the organization on a disciplined approach to planning. It calls on the organization to have a planning process in place, and conduct planning as a joint activity so that the myriad activities the various departments undertake can be better connected, coordinated, and interrelated. Planning puts an emphasis on ensuring that the strategies and actions delineated in Quadrant 1 drive service delivery and are not lost in the busy and complex day-to-day work. This is where the organization establishes meaning for the range of activities it engages in and ensures that its resources appropriately and equitably align to the overall vision and goals. Plans must include developing and building organizational capacity—both human and material—and managing data and communication.

- **Quadrant 1,** the design quadrant, focuses on developing the foundation for collaborative school reviews. It involves discussion about its tie to the vision, mission, and the district and establishes the vision for the school reviews. It sets measurable targets or outcomes for improvement, establishes policies, develops the design, and sets the procedures and protocols for the use of collaborative school reviews as a tool for improvement. The communication strategy and plan is a critical element for moving forward.

- **Quadrant 2,** the planning quadrant, focuses on planning the reviews—what needs to be put in place and how the process will unfold systemwide. It requires developing two distinct but related plans: a system plan and a school-specific plan. At the district level, it includes creating the implementation schedules and the actions that support alignment across the system. Time lines and roles or responsibilities for each review are identified and a plan is put in place for each school that involves the school's administration and staff. Capacity building, data management, and communication are components of each plan. Additionally, this quadrant establishes checkpoints for monitoring progress across the district to ensure effective management of the collaborative school review process and the timely resolution of issues and problems that may arise. Of particular importance is the plan for addressing issues impacting the whole district and which require a districtwide policy or direction.

(Continued)

Figure 1.3 (Continued)

- **Quadrant 3,** the implementation quadrant, focuses on implementing the collaborative school review process. It involves implementing the strategies and actions planned in Quadrant 2 and gathering and recording information or data. The critical elements are gathering and managing required data, following established processes and protocols, problem solving, maintaining relationships, communicating effectively, and sustaining momentum. At a system level, fidelity of implementation of the model is a key consideration.

- **Quadrant 4,** the securing accountability quadrant, focuses on monitoring the impact of collaborative school reviews as system improvement strategies. It includes data coding and analysis, as well as documenting, quantifying, and reporting outcomes. Critical are drawing conclusions and identifying corrective action, both for the school level and the district level. A key concern at the district level is maintaining momentum to ensure that the collaborative school reviews lead to improved outcomes. This is the monitoring function. It is necessary to evaluate the impacts of the collaborative school review process to determine its usefulness as a change management tool for the system and to identify any design adjustments to make it a more effective tool.

- **Quadrant 3** zeros in on the day-to-day delivery. It calls on the organization to be present, observant, and reflective. It emphasizes ensuring that clients are at the core of service delivery. This requires vigilance about the effective deployment of resources—both human and material—and attention to client needs and their levels of satisfaction with services received. If planning has occurred in Quadrant 2, the predictable can be effectively managed, leaving time and resources to both deal with the less predictable and more complex service delivery issues that will inevitably arise. A key concern is fidelity to the delivery model to ensure that what actually happens is what was intended in the design of the policy and the service delivery model.

- **Quadrant 4** focuses on results. It requires that the organization (1) clearly articulates an accountable structure; (2) has the data and monitoring system it needs to analyze its progress in the achievement of its vision, mandate, and goals; and (3) has the ability to take corrective action as required. It emphasizes the accountability structures and measurement systems that need to be in place. This includes both systematic data collection and analysis, which implies agreement about what data are to be collected, when, and how; and also designing, establishing, and managing processes, formats, and protocols for data management. The efficiency of the data collection system is particularly essential in this quadrant. The goal is to ensure an optimal level of data collected in the right formats and avoid an undue burden on the system. This quadrant highlights the need for aligned capacity building to ensure the achievement of system directions and goals. The analysis here centers upon ensuring efficacy of the strategies to meet the established goals—what gets monitored gets done.

change management process to systematically gather evidence and provide the analysis and mechanisms to decrease variability in practice, support positive accountability, and provide targeted and aligned capacity building. The goal is to enable schools and districts to move forward with a sense of purposeful urgency. The new focus on standards and the demands for increased accountability provide such an opportunity. One of the factors contributing to the variability in practice is discussed in Dan Lortie's (2002) research on teachers' workplace orientations; he identified "presentism," or short-term thinking as one impediment to sustained change. Another is the persistence of privatization, or to paraphrase, the individualized approach to teaching, where teachers refer to "their classroom and their students" and teaching is a closed door (Little, 1990). Targeted and intentional professional learning offer a learning organization a way to move collaboratively from the present—forward.

Collaborative school reviews, when tied to accountability, provide one vehicle for propelling an organization to collectively move into a new direction. Accountability can be seen as a positive driver when there is a shared acceptance of the data or evidence, along with an understanding and acceptance of the possible pathways to improving teaching and learning. Accountability is perceived negatively when it is punitive and staff sees themselves as victims and not as the agents of positive change. Collaborative school reviews provide a dynamic way out of this conundrum. The tension between needing to improve and actual improvement is often where change stalls. Collaborative school reviews provide a mechanism for all schools to be systematically reviewed. They lead to specific suggestions that pinpoint areas of improvement required to move the school along the continuum of improvement.

OUR CASE STUDY

The Lone Birch School District

The Lone Birch School District provides a case study to blend theory and effective practices and the use of evidence into practice. Lone Birch is a generic district, positioned in North America and an amalgam informed by our understanding about school systems in general and our suggestions framed within that knowledge. The discussion thus applies, with some adjustments, to any system anywhere. You will find that Lone Birch has many similarities to your school or district and that its experiences, albeit made-up, resonate with yours.

While examining Lone Birch, we use the phrase *looking in* when reflecting with the external lens of our own expertise; we use the phrase *thinking out* as a way to comment and make suggestions for your consideration.

Background

Schools and school systems are shaped by the culture, context, and capabilities of staff as well as students, parents, and the community. Our Lone Birch is a suburban North American school district of 25,000 students in fifty schools committed to school improvement. Its mission as reflected on its website is "All Students Achieve." Like most school systems, it is diverse in terms of wealth, educational attainment of parents, as well as race, language, and culture.

Like many districts, despite its mission statement and culture of good intentions, the student achievement results are inconsistent. Some schools are high performing and others have large numbers of students who are underachieving and failing to graduate. While the overall district student achievement results are slowly increasing, achievement gaps remain. Some of the achievement gaps appear to be tied to traditional sociodemographic indicators (poverty, English language learners [ELL], mobility, educational levels of parents); however, boys are underachieving in terms of literacy in affluent and less affluent areas. There are high-performing schools in lower socioeconomic and more culturally and linguistically diverse areas. For example, Pleasant Valley Elementary School, a JK–6 school with 400 students and situated in a lower sociodemographic and high ELL neighborhood, has shown improvement on student achievement indicators in the last two years. Meadows Middle School, a traditional school with 300 students in Grades 7–8, is not performing as well. Performance is stalled and the school has high suspension and failure rates. Harper High School, with over 800 students from a traditionally affluent area, is proud of its achievement record. These three will be the pilot schools used to demonstrate the application of collaborative school review processes.

Since Lea assumed the superintendent role four years ago, the emphasis districtwide has been improving student achievement, emphasizing outcomes in literacy and numeracy, and increasing the credit completion and graduation rates. Although pleased with Lone Birch's progress, the senior administration team and board members are frustrated with the inconsistent range in achievement results from student to student and school to school. The mission may be "All Students Achieve," but the reality is that many are not. The senior team recognizes the differences between and among schools in Lone Birch and they are asking, "How do we become more effective and consistent?" Their aim is for high quality and low variability across classrooms and across schools. Lea, in a speech to board members, references Marzano and Waters's (2009) findings from the Mid-continent Research in Education or McREL. They concluded that "high instructional quality with low variability among teachers is a hallmark of the world's best-performing education systems" (116).

The board members repeatedly ask: How do we go from good to great? What should be our pathway? There is the Lone Birch District Improvement Plan (LBDIP) and each school has created its own school improvement plan (SIP), in theory aligned to the central plan. The assistant superintendents of schools have reviewed the written SIPs, but plans have to be implemented and continuously monitored and revised. Lea often says "what gets monitored gets done." Improvement is happening but in pockets and not yet districtwide. She and her team are feeling the pressure from the board members, and also the public, to close gaps and demonstrate increased improvement. Lea's senior team is composed of her three associate superintendents as the supervisors of schools—Dante, Juan, and Katie—and the two central-assigned coordinating principals—Clay and Maria. All six are committed to raising the academic bar but they know to do so they also have to close the existing achievement gaps through changed classroom and school practices.

Two years ago, Lone Birch upgraded its student information collection system and increased the use of digital technologies in its schools. From her experience in a previous school district, Lea has brought her commitment to using data effectively—evidence informed decision making or EIDM. Lea wants to create a data tapestry of students' achievement, so Lone Birch is now gathering and using data from a multitude of sources including standardized assessments (in your jurisdiction they could be state, national, or provincial), credit completions, suspension, attendance, graduation, report cards, and attitudinal survey data to name a few. Data are disaggregated by gender, by students with special needs, and by ELL. These will become individual threads to be woven together in the tapestry. Lea was hoping the last set of high-stakes assessments would show a greater degree of improvement across the underperforming schools as a result of the district's change initiatives, but that didn't happen consistently. The bar is rising in Lone Birch but achievement gaps remain.

Like many districts, Lone Birch faces declining enrollments and decreasing budgets. Lea understands this means she and her team must be more strategic in their approach, given the fiscal restraints. The public wants evidence of improvement, but what to emphasize and what to discontinue? How can Lea and her team really know how they can strategically impact achievement in all schools and classrooms within Lone Birch?

Lea and her team gather to discuss the current district improvement plan, which will require revisions the following year. Key questions include: What is really happening in our schools in terms of teaching and learning? What do the data say? What data tapestry is created? More specifically, the team acknowledges the need to address the following:

- Are the Lone Birch directions being effectively implemented across schools? Is the intended really happening? What are our indicators, or look-fors, of success?

- Are the current professional development (PD) sessions we supported at the district and at the school level paying off? Is pedagogy deepening and practice changing in the classrooms? Has instructional leadership improved and become more intentional and focused?

- How can we help reduce the variation and increase the quality across our schools?

- How are we as a senior management team really impacting student achievement? How can we become more responsive and effective?

Lea tries to be in at least one school every two weeks but sometimes these feel like staged events. As superintendent, she worries: Does she really know what is happening beyond her campus visits, conversations with administrators, and reports from the schools' supervisors? Lone Birch has some data sets, but she needs the data tapestry to have a clearer idea of regular classroom practice. What could or should she and her team be doing differently? She knows that the schools that were not achieving to expectations are frustrated too. Some are experiencing resistance to further change. She wonders: Is she pushing too hard or moving too fast, or not hard and fast enough?

Katie and Clay have attended a presentation on collaborative school reviews and now wonder if this process could provide some of the answers to the questions Lea has posed. They share what they heard, and Lea asks that they present to all of senior administration. After much discussion, the senior team agrees to proceed and consider a pilot for collaborative school reviews. Piloting before scaling up is the Lone Birch way of implementing change and they have used this option with other systemwide initiatives. Lea reminds the team that improving schools is neither simple nor for the fainthearted. Change comes with opportunities and risks.

Reader Reflections

Is the Lone Birch senior team asking the right questions?

Are these the types of questions you are asking in your own school or district?

What areas of challenge do you currently face?

What is your experience with variability between classes and schools?

How are you monitoring progress in each school and across schools?

What is the monitoring telling you?

Thinking Out

Effective schools are reliant on effective staff. To decrease variation and increase quality, the research indicates that the system leadership needs to create the conditions to promote and sustain the instructional leadership of school-based administrators (principals, head teachers) and their teaching staffs. The focus must be an intentional, aligned, and coordinated approach to change. Collaborative school reviews are designed to provide just that. System leaders can establish the joint direction, shared vision, and understanding required for engagement in the improvement process. Setting collective goals can develop teamwork, common focus on continuous improvement, and feelings of self and collective efficacy. Developing the collective capacity across the system enables change to move forward consistently and with a shared sense of urgency. To actualize measureable goals and targets requires data systems to gather, aggregate, disaggregate, monitor, and analyze student achievement data to provide the accountability structure. Effective systems require all of these components working seamlessly and interchangeably. School and system improvement is like rocket science—it is complex, multilayered, and reliant on research and best practices. Effective leaders strategically seize the moment to bring about improvement while building collective capacity. How are collaborative school reviews situated within the school and school-system effectiveness effort?

Where to begin? What should come first?

These areas are addressed in the next chapter.

Reader Reflections

Do you know that in many American states, the corrections department examines the number of students reading on grade level for Grades 2–4 to predict the number of prison spaces they will require? (Bernhardt, 2004)

If educational data can inform the building of prisons, surely it can be used to inform and improve the practice of teaching and learning.

IN SUMMARY

Collaborative school reviews differ from typical school reviews in a number of critical ways:

- They are anchored on a collaborative model that includes schools in the planning and implementation of the review.

- They are embodied within a high level of accountability.
- Staff capacity building is a core goal and strategy.
- Continuous improvement powers the process.

As we proceed, Lone Birch will be used throughout this guide to illustrate the application of the concept. This real-life situation provides a practical example of why and how collaborative school reviews might be implemented in your schools and districts.

 For further information and additional resources, please visit the website associated with this book at www.collaborativeschoolreviews.com.

2 Designing Collaborative School Reviews

M ike Borgfijord (2012), superintendent of the Seine River School
Division in Manitoba, Canada, asserts that "school reviews are an
integral component of building learning communities that demand higher
standards for student learning."

DESIGNING EFFECTIVELY

Our tendency is to spend our time in day-to-day implementation and routine
activities, what we call Quadrant 3 or the delivery quadrant. As educators,
we sometimes jump in and solve problems without first doing the work to
ensure we have the proper direction, structure, and resourcing in place to
achieve our goals. Or we may focus on a specific aspect of reform and not
think systemically. Remember, for strategic improvement, it's not single
initiatives of improvement but the weaving together of system improvements in a coherent and sustainable manner that make the difference for
all students. The lack of effective design and planning can lead to solutions
that have not been fully thought out and adapted to take into account the
specific system needs and context. There is much evidence of unintended
results from rash implementation of strategies and processes that, while

effective in some jurisdictions, may not work in other jurisdictions in the same intended way.[1]

Quadrant 1 of our strategic lens calls for a methodical and thoughtful analysis and design before moving to planning and implementation (see Figure 2.1). It is one of the features that differentiates our conceptual model. It is Step 1 in a strategic change management process, and provides the touchstones to be taken into account as part of the conceptualization and design of a collaborative school review process that can be applied across the district or at an independent school. This attention up front to the design issues to customize the process helps ensure sustainability of any changes ensuing from the reviews.

Quadrant 1, in this strategic management framework, deals with broader design issues: the district's policies, overall strategic directions, and range of improvement programs. For our purposes, we have narrowed this potentially broad scope of strategic change management and focused it on the design of collaborative school reviews. In this first step of developing the design, you will need to achieve the following:

- Link the collaborative school reviews to district vision, mission, and transformational agenda.
- Create collaborative school review policy.

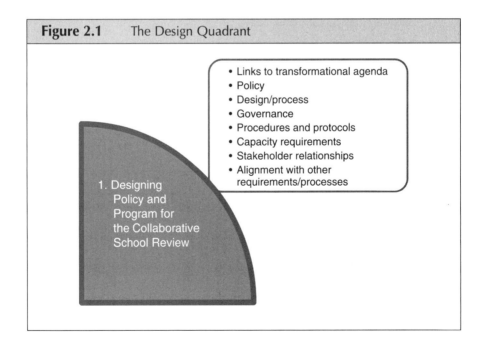

Figure 2.1   The Design Quadrant

- Links to transformational agenda
- Policy
- Design/process
- Governance
- Procedures and protocols
- Capacity requirements
- Stakeholder relationships
- Alignment with other requirements/processes

1. Designing Policy and Program for the Collaborative School Review

---

[1]In Bev's former district, when the boys were not including enough detail in their answers on the provincial assessments, they began a campaign of having them fill in the box provided for the short-answer responses. The following year, after analyzing the results, they had to go back and say "don't write bigger but add detail and depth to your answers" and spend time teaching boys the why and how of comprehensive responses.

- Create collaborative school review process.
- Establish governance.
- Develop procedures and protocols.
- Analyze and address capacity requirements.
- Engage stakeholders in the process.
- Align with other requirements and processes.

How do you design an effective collaborative school review process for your district? Begin with the end goal in mind and map backward.

Link Collaborative School Reviews to District Vision, Mission, and Transformational Agenda

We view the collaborative school review process as a transformational change strategy and, as such, it needs to tie to your district's overall vision and mission, as well as your agenda to improve student achievement across all schools in the district. The real value of collaborative school reviews is garnered when they are contextualized and institutionalized within the district's overall improvement effort.

Conceptualization needs to occur at the district level. The state, province, or region can set parameters, guidelines, and mandates but the contextualization must be custom crafted to incorporate the unique needs, culture, and climate of the district. In addition, the specifics of each individual school need to be factored in. Barber, Moffit, and Kihn (2010) identified two components critical to change: the system leader who is the formal leader in a K–12 system; and the delivery leader who is designated by the system's formal leader to head the initiative, see it through to completion, and who is, in turn, supported by a local team. Our design for collaborative school reviews provides for both of these roles.

The design needs to take into account other key district strategies and programs and tactics. These context-based variables need to be systemically addressed in the design of the school review. The design component must include developing specific policies to guide the use of collaborative school reviews as well as procedures and protocols to support an efficient and consistent review process across the system. This includes schedules and planning cycles as well as formats.

Establish Clear and Shared Expectations and Directions for Student Achievement and School Improvement

A prerequisite for effective change is clarity about what you want to achieve through the change effort and why you are selecting a specific change strategy. That clarity needs to include how to determine the level of success of the change effort. Without such clarity, you cannot know if the change strategy has been effective. In education, our core goal is increasing student achievement while closing achievement gaps. This goal must apply to all schools and all students and not just some schools and the fortunate few. All systems have some schools that understand and excel but the reality is that not all schools within a school system share the same levels of effectiveness. There should be a clear pathway and indicators to identify where each school is along a common continuum of improvement. System- and school-level strategies and resources must move each school from where it is on the continuum toward the articulated desired goal. The concept of continuous change is another non-negotiable. The system needs to set the directions, resources, and targets. The district must tightly hold this aspect of the change process for the system.

Collaborative school reviews provide a mechanism to identify where each school is and to provide suggestions for improvement to move schools along the improvement continuum, while respecting both equity and equality. They provide a vehicle to set this in motion. They can be used to establish clear expectations and directions for student achievement and school improvement at the district level and also to establish the accountability framework to monitor, measure, and report the change so that the movement can be tracked at the school level as well. The process provides transparency and requires establishing a shared vision of high expectations for students that both raises the academic bar and closes achievement gaps. We know that systems can only work on a few explicit improvement targets at the same time: too many and the focus is diffuse and nothing ever really gets implemented. People become cynical or frustrated or both. Collaborative school reviews ensure that change is focused, manageable, and sustainable. The aim is for a clear and unrelenting focus on improved achievement that stakeholders widely share, whether at the school system or school level. This must be unambiguous and non-negotiable. Few is better—aim for thin strategic improvement plans, not thick ones that are never implemented. Improving achievement for all by raising the bar and closing gaps is our core purpose.

Build a Data Tapestry to Achieve Evidence-Informed Practice

In Chapter 1, we discussed the use of data as a tapestry. It is woven from different data sets, layered, and based on different perspectives. When referencing the collective use of data, we use the term *data tapestry* to be evocative of the richness of the data that the review will encompass. A data tapestry of a school or district weaves different strands or multiple data sets and measures together to form a visual picture of achievement. Data are critical to improvement—what is measured becomes the focus. To further illustrate, Sharratt and Fullan (2009) write about the need for intelligent accountability. Accountability relies on data and metrics. The district requires an effective and efficient way to gather and manage data and provide schools with relevant and disaggregated data about their performance. The data inform practice by providing opportunities for educators using collaborative structures to unpack and make sense of the evidence. Evidence without changed practice is not effective use of system time and resources, and can be counterproductive. Data are addressed in greater detail in Chapter 3.

ESTABLISHING A COLLABORATIVE SCHOOL REVIEW POLICY

We recommend that the district begin with establishing a policy for using collaborative school reviews as a strategic change management strategy. By *policy,* we mean the overarching purpose, parameters, and framework that will guide the design and implementation of the collaborative school review process for the district. It is important that the policy be written and that it articulates the "shalls" for collaborative school reviews. The policy needs to specify what will be tightly held centrally and what will be more loosely devolved to schools. The policy institutionalizes the review process and ensures that the parameters and requirements are clear.

Clarity about the review process allows staff to understand the following three elements: (1) the purpose of collaborative school review and how this purpose relates to learning for all students, (2) the process and time line, and (3) the protocols that will be followed.

Designing the collaborative school review process is an opportunity to bring order to the collection of disparate and shifting reform initiatives that are typical of systems undergoing major reform. The design phase provides a vehicle for aligning the various initiatives and directions so as to achieve a more coherent, intentional, and well-supported approach. The goal in this quadrant is to clearly articulate the process of the collaborative school review, and to explicitly connect the review to what else is happening in the system. Think of system coherence. Look at the various initiatives and directions your system or school has and their connections to ensure they are aligned. This may require realignment and even dropping some. You need to then make sure that these initiatives are rationalized, organized, and communicated.

The design phase should facilitate this examination of the priorities, the range of interventions, and the host of strategies that have been established to increase student achievement.

We recommend that your written policy address the following components:

- Statement of the purpose of school reviews and the relationship to the learning agenda for the district
- Identification of the areas of focus and alignment to the larger improvement plan or structure
- Definition of scope and clarification of expectations
- Set of goals that connect to the existing student success targets
- Identification of the locus of responsibility for the school review process (member of senior administration) who can act as the team leader
- Outline of the expectations for the system and for the schools
- Outline of the roles and responsibilities of the system and the school-based participants
- Mandate for interdepartmental coordination, with resource allocation specified, including release time for capacity building as well as planning for the school, external review teams, and time lines
- Clarification for the process to be consistently applied across schools within a district and school system
- Key requirements that must be met for conducting the reviews, including the use of data, participation, and the documentation and use of findings
- Application of the policy to all schools
- Requirement for an external review team(s) composed of experts in the process
- Mandatory training for the external team(s) and capacity building for all participants
- Specification of the types of data to be used as evidence and its management
- Recognition and accounting for costs in implementation
- Requirement for an observational component of instructional space including classrooms
- Delineation of the areas to be addressed and reported in the review process, and how the results will be used
- Requirement for clear and strategic communication to the stakeholders

Goals, Leadership, and Accountability

In the design stage, we recommend focusing only on a small number of shared and measureable goals that will impact learning to frame the collaborative school review. These goals must tie to the district improvement plan. You will also want to build strong leadership supportive of improvement. The system and delivery leaders must be seen to champion and be involved in the review process, and be able to communicate the key messages. Additionally, the district must uphold accountability for improving student learning. If schools are not accountable, then pressures to improve for all students will not become an instrument of change. Schools will revert to their comfort level that good is good enough, or that it is the students' or parents' fault. Demographics are no longer acceptable as the rationalization for the lack of progress in student achievement, for there are too many examples of improving schools situated in challenging communities (Hilliard, 1998; Reeves, 2005). Such rationalizations ignore the power and value-added contributions of teachers and administrators.

An additional check is to look at your statistical neighbors or "like schools and districts." You can benefit from benchmarking your situation to other comparable jurisdictions. When we are leading program reviews at a state, provincial, or district level, we always benchmark best practices in comparable districts.

Expectations for Schools

Think about what will be tightly held and non-negotiable and what is loosely held and in the individual school's purview. As part of the design process, consider how you will select the schools in terms of cycle of involvement. Will it be volunteers or will the schools be selected based on specified criteria? What has been your past practice? If the practice has been effective, then keep it. If the schools have choice in terms of when they will be reviewed, remember to clarify in policy that all schools will be part of the process. We maintain that no school can self-select out.

We suggest that the schools choose the focus areas that matter for their individual reviews. These focus areas must align with your systemwide directions.

How the school prepares for the collaborative school review can be a school-based decision. This focuses the school component of the review process on the role of the principal and the school improvement team at the school level. It will be their role to organize and prepare the school. Remember to include the supervisor of the school who can provide a safety net if something goes wrong with the process. How the school staff will be involved can be a school-based decision, but the parameters should be stated in the policy and design including how they as a faculty will be made aware of the policy, procedures, and protocols. This process makes use of existing structures and so should not incur additional expenses.

The system needs to ensure alignment in terms of communication from the superintendent and from the principal so messages are consistent. We recognize that communication has to be customized to the school's culture, and should include a strategy to deal with resistance.

To enable participant readiness throughout the system, groundwork must occur early in the process. This means that senior management and school-based administrators must have the capacity to lead this process.

If they cannot, then capacity building for administrators needs to occur as a prerequisite to implementing the process.

Another design consideration for schools is the assumption that all instructional and learning spaces, or the instructional environment, will be part of the review. We suggest these include all instructional spaces such as libraries, resource areas, gyms, technology labs, art rooms, music and drama rooms, science labs, and so forth. The exception might be specific self-contained classes that address the needs of students with complex behavior, anger management, and mental health issues where having external visitors could be a danger to students and others in the class. This is where context and good judgment matter.

Anticipate probable problem areas. In particular, decisions should be made about whether to include supply or occasional teachers, and faculty of education or preservice teachers, as part of the review process and protocols. This might be an area for consultation with the teachers' union or federation or associations if this is part of your regular practice. Context matters. The protocols arising from the design need to be clearly and strategically communicated to the system.

Cycle for School Reviews

Think of reviews as requiring a three- to five-year cycle. That will help determine how many schools need to be reviewed in a single year. In a smaller district of less than thirty schools, the district may want ten per year and use a three-year cycle.[2] The review cycle ensures that every school is reviewed on a timely basis, that the school is given an opportunity to implement change, and that there is a visible commitment to the continuous improvement nature of the school review process. In the design, aim for a mix of elementary, middle, and secondary or high schools. In terms of alignment, it makes sense to link what is happening in elementary and middle schools to the initiatives at the feeder or partner high schools, which should align with district priorities.

Once the reviews have been completed, remember in the analysis to look at patterns and trends across elementary and secondary panels. This may create a need for more interactive conversations and planning across the two panels to bring about improvement. You should also align the collaborative school reviews with your district improvement plan cycle.

Initially, for the first round of reviews, you may want to consider pilot or volunteer schools. We suggest one volunteer school per family of schools or at least one elementary, middle (if you have one), and high school in the initial round. After the first year, placement in terms of the cycle can

---

[2]In the Toronto District School Board (TDSB), with over 500 schools, over 100 district reviews occur per year.

be negotiated between the family of schools supervisor and the individual schools. Look to mix schools that are performing well with underperforming schools in each cycle. If you just leave it to the schools, schools whose achievement is less than the district's norm may be resistant and choose not to volunteer. This is something we have experienced. These schools may need to be "voluntold." The need for the cycle is to be clear, but also flexible; sometimes a crisis will occur—deaths, tragedies—and the timetable has to be revised. Anticipate issues in the design component and this will assist in a more effective implementation.

Time in School

In our design, the external team needs only to stay one day for the onsite visit in the school under review; however the onsite visit could last two days. Because the members of the review team are all internal to the district they can be replaced for the day with no additional costs for staffing.[3] Frame the day to align with the school's own timetable. These details are more extensively discussed in Chapters 4, 5, and 6 as we follow Lone Birch and the schools.

Another consideration is the length of time the external review team members will spend observing in individual classrooms. Consider an allocation of fifteen to twenty-five minutes per class, which includes five minutes for the two team members observing the class to step out of the room to write and debrief. Based on the timetable there is a need to ensure that every instructional space is visited at least once. Fifteen to twenty minutes in a class allows for detailed observations if the observation lens is clearly focused and structured. Design strategically and execute flexibly. For example, in the design, build in some days for inclement weather. We remember reviews being cancelled because of snow.

The total size of the team depends on the number of teachers or classrooms that require observation. We clarify this point in Chapter 3. Also, because observational data gathering is a key skill for the review team, this needs to be a component in the training sessions and protocols developed for classroom observations.

Membership of the School Review Teams

The design needs to specify who is to be involved in the collaborative school review process and then establish the structure for how and when

---

[3]Most schools have staff designated in a position of responsibility if the administrator is away. Use this as a leadership opportunity for assistant or vice principals. Single administrator schools may require a supply principal for the day, which would be an additional cost. If so, build this into the budget.

staff will participate in reviews. At the system level, collaborative school review teams are established to conduct the external reviews. The external teams should comprise a mix of existing system and school-based staff. Unlike an audit, we recommend using existing personnel to avoid additional costs of contracting external staff. It is a matter of reallocating personnel. School-based administrators can serve on one or two reviews so their time in their existing school doesn't need to be compromised. If you have the capacity, consider designating some members of the team as permanent members across all the reviews as a way to build coherency and expertise across the various school reviews. This is not a full-time position but added as part of other duties. What can be removed from their existing portfolio to minimize costs? Some districts include teachers who are consultants, or literacy or numeracy coaches, and other districts may involve only centrally assigned or school-based administrators due to concerns of teachers being in other teachers' classrooms and being seen in an evaluative light. The team should reflect the context of the school. If possible, the external team should include some members with specialized expertise in areas such as special education, English language learners (ELL), early literacy, and issues of equity such as gender and culture (if that is a focus area of the school under review and if you have the capacity). In larger districts, members of departments such as research, safe and secure schools, equity, special education, and technology departments may be included too. Again, context matters. Use your existing expertise.

The size of the team should be based on the number of students and teachers in the school under review. The larger the school population, the larger the review team needs to be. Large high schools of 1,500 or more students may require sixteen to twenty-four people to ensure all instructional spaces are visited. Small elementary schools of less than 200 students may only need a team of four to six members. The review may not last the entire school day in a small school. Our rule of thumb is at least two team members for each classroom visit. The focused conversations after each observation assist with interrater reliability and help to build expertise across the district and to promote "accountable talk" among and between members of the team.

It is helpful to have one experienced and one less experienced staff member on each team. Think about the possibilities for coaching and mentorship. You also need to develop depth and build the capacity of younger administrators. Consider school administrators who have had a review and ones whose schools are anticipating a review. Try and have the lead(s) common across all of the reviews so there is reliability and consistency in the approaches and in the written reports. Smaller systems may have only one lead who coordinates and writes all of the reports. This can occur by reprioritizing the job descriptions of existing centrally assigned staff. Large systems with more than fifty schools may want multiple leads for a district with several hundreds of thousands to a million students. The number of external review team leads depends on context and the size of the district. Think of this as an opportunity to build expertise, for what the review teams will be involved in provides invaluable insights on what is happening, how things might be improved, and the strategies that could achieve the improvement. These decisions should be made as part of the planning component for the onsite component, which we discuss in the next chapter. Remember in the design, to plan for the inclusion of a supply list of reviewers to accommodate illnesses and emergency situations.

At the school level, an improvement team led by the school-based administrators (principal, head teacher, vice or assistant principal) is the norm in our experience. The roles and responsibilities of the school-based improvement team should be outlined in the governance component of the design phase. It is easiest to use an existing school-based structure, so in your district it might be the department chairs or leadership teams. Aligning to existing school structures makes the process less disjointed and more familiar for staff. Allow the focus of the schools to help shape the composition of the team. As the process unfolds, principals and assistant or vice principals whose schools have been reviewed should be included on future external review teams. This builds joint ownership and respects the role of principals as school leaders. As one principal said, "This was the best PD. I learned tons and now understand the intention and would have prepared my school for the review differently."

Governance

There needs to be a clear structure in place regarding roles and responsibilities during the review process. These include locus of responsibility and management of the review process.

Where will the locus of responsibility reside?

We recommend that there be a clear chain of command to senior management and that a system person be assigned the responsibility with the appropriate authority, credibility, experiences, and resources to manage the collaborative school review process. You will also have to report to the board members. The system may select a team leader who could be a coordinating administrator. In smaller districts, the team leader for collaborative school reviews may be one of the senior system leaders. This will depend on local realities. The senior management should have positional authority and the team leader should have operational authority. In all cases, the designated team leader for collaborative school reviews will be accountable for the process as it evolves and for coordinating with others. This would thus be the go-to person who will provide the links from the review committee to senior administration and likely provide strategic communication and support during the reviews.

Managing the Process

Consider establishing a cross-department reference group or working team to shape the design and planning process so that all stakeholders are consulted, share, and have a role in the process. Their roles and responsibilities should be described for clarity. Membership will depend on the size of the district, the number of departments, and the local context. The reference groups may include members of the following, depending on the district:

- Operations, human resources (HR), finance, facilities, technology, or research
- Representatives from teaching and learning, such as coordinators, coaches, and consultants
- Representatives from the school leaders or principals' councils (may require an elementary and a secondary representative)
- Teachers' organizations, depending on local context, if this type of consultation is part of the existing culture (might be the union or federation)

This cross-department reference group is operational and will assist in the design and logistics as well as provide ongoing input. A system process needs to pay attention to resourcing and coordination. This team can assist with effective communication because they will all report back to their various stakeholders or departments. The reference group may elect to establish subgroups to look at effective practices and research options for the design. Often responsibility for technology may reside in these operations, HR, or in another department. Technology departments will often have a major responsibility for data gathering and, sometimes, analysis. If there are to be any recommendations regarding these types of system structures, or if there are budget or staffing implications because of release time, those responsible should be included on the planning committee. The roles, responsibilities, and expectations for the leadership and participants on the review teams need to be clarified.

As part of the governance structure, the responsibility for monitoring the results of the collaborative school review process and the efficacy of the design needs to be assigned. This ensures the process delivers the desired results. This should include a mechanism to revise the policy and design as required. Also designate responsibility for reporting the results publicly.

Checklist for Governance Structure

We recommend developing clearly articulated expectations, roles, and responsibilities for the following:

- Senior management
- Designated school review lead
- A cross-departmental reference or work group
- The external review team(s)
- The internal school improvement teams
- Monitoring and evaluation of the school review policy and process

Procedures and Protocols

The parameters for conducting collaborative school reviews, and for ensuring that the process is ethical as well as respectful of how the district typically conducts its business, need to also be reflected in how the school reviews will be conducted. Protocols form the rules for implementation and must be clearly articulated, communicated, and understood. They need to be contextual to the district depending on issues such as culture, historical precedent, and issues with the various bargaining groups. This includes issues of privacy, confidentiality, and choice to participate. The protocols need to provide clear statements in terms of who will do what and how. For example, the protocols need to specify what information will be recorded the day of the onsite visit and by whom. The protocols need to delineate (1) when observational notes will be taken during classroom observations and the format for those notes, (2) whether or not attendance at the initial briefing at the school and the debriefing session at the end of the review will be voluntary or mandatory, and (3) time lines and expectations for producing the written report and distributing the findings. The templates and forms to document and record need to be designed and consistently applied. To make the process clear and transparent, we suggest that these be developed in a collaborative arrangement recognizing stakeholder relationships and requirements. Consideration could be given to having the key questions and answers (Q&A) recorded and posted on the intranet of the district's website. Schools anticipating reviews can then search the Q&A and issues can be avoided proactively.

Conflicts generally arise when people either unintentionally or willfully stray from the established protocols. For instance, in one review Bev was involved with, although members of the review were told to "turn their

BlackBerries off," some members were texting and responding to e-mail and text messages while they were observing teachers' classes. On another, members of the external review team inappropriately shared confidential information. Clear and explicit expectations therefore need to be set for review team members. There also needs to be a backup plan with staff designed to fill in if needed. The review process can be seriously impacted when designated members of the review team do not show up the day of the review.

In the absence of feedback, learning is challenging even with motivation (Marzano, Frontier, & Livingston, 2011). Feedback is thus an integral component of reviews. It should be purposeful and appropriate. Feedback in our process occurs formally in the verbal debrief of the initial findings at the end of the day of the onsite school visit, and in the written report that follows. It also occurs informally as faculties engage in conversations at their school about their practice and in the discussions that likely will arise from the reviews. The feedback mirrors where they are on the continuum of change. The school improvement team can use the feedback to monitor ongoing progress at the school level. We discuss this in depth as we proceed through the Lone Birch case study. Reviews offer schools explicit descriptive feedback on their efforts to improve achievement.

STRUCTURE AND FLOW FOR THE REVIEW

We have suggested that your protocols specify the structure and flow of the review. The school improvement or review team at the school level can begin planning for the review as soon as the process is confirmed, even before individual schools are identified for a collaborative review. There should also be a meeting structure with specific expectations and descriptors set for each of these meetings (see Figure 2.2). The protocols should include direction to the supervisor or superintendent about his or her role and responsibility in overseeing these meetings. In large districts, there may be several school supervisors, and in smaller districts perhaps just one. In some cases, it may be the department of education or the ministry with supervisory control.

The flow and time frame for the actual review at the individual school needs to be based around the length of the school day. Typically, the external review team will arrive around 8:00 a.m. or earlier to meet staff in a large common space, such as the library or staff room. This gives the team and teaching staff time to mingle and introduce themselves before classes begin. Often, coffee and optional nutritious snacks may be provided during a meet-and-greet session as the external team is formally introduced. In our experience, sharing food can also help alleviate some of the inherent tensions.

Figure 2.2   Designated Meetings for the Review

Meeting	Time/Location/Attendees	Date	Notes
A premeeting with the individual school improvement team and the school's supervisor to discuss the focus for the upcoming review and the evidence to be presented			
A premeeting with the members of the individual external review team prior to the onsite visit (this can also be a virtual meeting) to prepare for the onsite visit to the designated school			
A debrief of the school's administrative staff before the verbal feedback at the end of the school visit			
A verbal feedback to staff at the end of the review day			
A debrief meeting with the school improvement team to present the findings and suggestions that form the written report			
A meeting following the school's unpacking of the written report, with the supervisor at the school to monitor how the opportunities for improvement are being implemented			
A meeting to present the system findings and recommendations, once the first group of reviews are complete, to the board members and the public			

This should be a system budget item, because the costs of providing food during the day of the review should not fall on the school to absorb.[4] This may not be necessary in a small district where everyone knows one another, but it is still a way to create comfort before the actual review begins. This is a strategy to respond to your unique culture.

Following the introduction of the external review team, there should be a planned presentation by the internal school team to set the context and highlight some key information about the school. To avoid long presentations, consider directing schools to prepare a short, pithy presentation of approximately fifteen to twenty minutes. It should not be self-congratulatory but rather emphasize what is really important to know about the school. This component is loosely held and in the purview of the school under review. These presentations can be gathered and used in board meetings or for the school's or district's marketing. We expand on the issue of school-created presentations in Chapter 4.

Following the school's presentation, the team will need some time component to plan for the classroom observations. The first observation should begin approximately ten minutes after classes begin. This allows for teachers to settle their classes and begin the learning process. In some jurisdictions, you may select to begin observations as soon as the classes enter. Either way, our recommendation is to specify your decisions in the design to avoid misunderstandings later. The schedule should designate three to five classes per team for observation and then at least a thirty-minute break for the review team to debrief and share their initial observations. The ensuing discussions about what was observed and the evidence gathered helps establish interrater reliability and shared learning. One member of the review team should be tasked with keeping notes for the group. It makes most sense for the team lead to be that designate. Consider how you can use technology to assist in note-taking during the review. More specific discussion of how the process can unfold will occur as we follow Lone Birch working its way through the process.

In a small school, as mentioned earlier, the onsite visit may only last a half a day, but most onsite visits last until the end of formal instructional time. The external review team will need some time in the schedule to begin to consolidate their findings and prepare the verbal feedback due at the end of the school day. Once the verbal feedback in terms of preliminary findings and a few suggestions for improvement are composed, we suggest you then debrief the school's administrative staff (principal and vice or assistant principal) to share the findings and begin to strategize the verbal feedback session. This respects their role as instructional leaders as well as leaders within the broader district.

---

[4]If one of the high schools has a catering program, use that for the food requirements. It's good for students and is cost effective; if budgets are too tight, then provide just coffee, tea, and water.

Next, a verbal feedback session should be provided for staff approximately ten to fifteen minutes after student dismissal to allow teachers time to regroup, yet not impact their end-of-day plans too much. In the design, consider whether this session will be voluntary or mandatory, and think about similar types of meetings that occur in your district. In our experience, the preliminary feedback session at the end of the day should be voluntary. Most staff members, we have found, will attend. The school's supervisor or the team leader can conduct the verbal debrief. We walk you through this process in depth, again using Lone Birch, in the proceeding chapters.

PROTOCOLS FOR CLASSROOM OBSERVATIONS

We all know that having others in your classroom as you teach can be stressful. Having members of the external team or any other adult in the classroom can, for some teachers, be even more stressful. In our experience, some teachers are unnerved by a review team writing during the classroom observation as they are teaching, while others are not bothered. Either way, the aim is to minimize disruptions for the teacher and the students. A key component of instructional leadership is purposeful classroom visibility. The more those school-based administrators are purposefully visible in classrooms, the less likely the stress will be for teachers. If there is an expectation and a culture of purposeful classroom visibility, then both the external review team and the classroom teachers will be comfortable with the protocols. In our experience, classroom visibility for administrators is a non-negotiable. It enables administrators to assess coherency of practice across classrooms, to monitor initiatives underway in the school, to observe teaching and learning, and then to use the data to provide collegial feedback to staff as part of the learning continuum toward improvement. We know, however, that this is not necessarily a regular practice in all districts. You will need to gauge this as part of your planning. If this is not a regular practice in your district, consider ways to build school-based and system-based administrator capacity in purposeful classroom observations as part of the preparation for implementing your collaborative school review process.

Classroom observations are Bev's passion and forte. Training in how and what to observe and how to provide meaningful feedback will help administrators build a sense of comfort with this aspect of the review process. You might consider one of the following: instructional rounds, the Three-Minute Walk-Through, power walks, learning walks, diagnostics, or instructional walks. Find the one best suited to your district's culture and style. Whenever possible, align yours to your existing effective practices. Explicit classroom observation protocols developed in consultation with key stakeholders will help alleviate some of the anxiety and possible resistance.

Expectations and Protocols
for the Onsite Classroom Observations

The following list provides suggested content for developing protocols:

- *Uphold confidentiality.* Do not name teachers or share information about what was observed. Issues of confidentiality need to be front and center in your protocols. We have seen trust dissipate when information was inappropriately leaked or discussed.

- *Limit classroom observations to fifteen to twenty minutes.* If you are not writing during the classroom observation, build in the time to write once you leave the classroom. Build in time (five minutes) to debrief, share, and get to the next classroom.

- *Give teachers some measure of control.* Teachers should have the option of introducing the members of the external review team to students or ignoring them and continuing with the lesson plan.

- *Reinforce that classroom observations are nonevaluative events.* The communication strategy and protocols should continually emphasize that the focus is on learning and the external review team looks for patterns and trends. No reference is to be made to a specific classroom or teacher, but rather all descriptions generalized into none, a few, some, many, and all.

- *Uphold classrooms as constructs of learning space.* The resources, manipulatives, reading materials, computers, and other technology will form part of the observational lens of the review.

- *Use the resources and materials posted on the walls and on chart paper to form part of the analysis.* These posted materials involve teaching and learning—"walls and halls talk." Classrooms are a learning environment. Are learning goals or learning targets posted? Think about cuing systems—are there anchor charts, rubrics, student work, word walls, exemplars, and success criteria? If so, what are the key messages? Are there common cuing systems in the school that you see from class to class such as messaging on inferencing, responding, summarizing, nonfiction, prediction, ecology, bullying, or problem solving? Remember that you are more likely to see cuing systems used more frequently in classrooms for the elementary panel; in middle schools and high schools, teachers share classrooms and rotate from class to class and so may be reluctant to post these types of cuing systems. Sometimes these walls can feel barren and institutional, yet learners need cuing systems—it is essential for some and good for all and will form part of the direction resulting from implementing the CCSS.

- *Ensure that learning is visibly and jointly owned in classrooms.* What is the visual evidence of student involvement in the learning? Consider whether the posted cuing systems—anchor charts, exemplars—are commercially prepared and bought by the teacher, teacher-created, or cocreated with students. Who owns the work? What should be the ratio of teacher-created and teacher-bought materials to student work? Why?

● *Remember that how teachers arrange their classrooms can be indicative of learning.* Are desks grouped or in rows? Are groupings fixed or flexible? Is there evidence of cooperative group strategies in use or are students working together without a structure?

● *Prepare for student interaction.* If the class is teacher-led, then the members of the external review team may just observe and not ask questions of students or may quietly examine their work. If students are working independently or interdependently in groups, members of the review team may ask them questions. The teachers should be told that members of the team will be asking their students some questions and scanning their work. Specific suggestions for questions to ask students are noted in the next section.

● *Ensure that there is a scan of students' notebooks, journals, and materials.* These give an indication of the learning. Pay attention to teacher feedback: Is it descriptive? Is it timely? Is it motivational and corrective? Do you see evidence of assessment for learning or is it mainly assessment of learning? A scan of student work will give you insights into what is being stressed in the classroom. Yet be sensitive to your culture; in some jurisdictions this may be viewed as too intrusive. Remember the purpose is to move the learning agenda forward. That is why this needs to be specified in the protocols. In some jurisdictions scanning students' work and notebooks may be seen as too high-stakes. This is why these potentially problematic issues are important to address in the design section. Again, context matters.

Possible Questions for Members of the Review Team to Ask Students

Based on our experiences, the questions that follow represent the types of questions that members of the external review team may ask students.

1. *What are you learning?* (You may need to ask probing questions of students to find the specific objectives, learning goals, learning targets, or expectations.)

2. *Why is it important for your teacher to be teaching you this skill or concept or why is it important that you learn it? How does it help you understand the learning goal or target?*

3. *Do you find this task easy or hard? What makes a task easy or hard?*

4. *If you aren't sure of the answer or response the teacher wants, where in the classroom might you find the information?* (i.e., anchor charts, rubrics, exemplars and cuing systems, other students, dictionary, the Web, Google, the teacher)

5. *Do you know how to improve the quality of your work?* (i.e., rubric, success criteria) *How can you improve the quality of your work? Who can help?*

6. (If students are reading) *Who selected the reading material?* (i.e., is it whole class, do students choose, is it selected texts for guided practice) *Do you enjoy the book? Why? What makes a book enjoyable?* (There are gender considerations to reading and writing.)

7. (If students are working in groups) *Who selected the groups? How often do they change? Do you see evidence of cooperative group structures in place?* (i.e., do students have assigned tasks and specific responsibilities in the group?)

8. (If students are watching another student or groups of students present) *Do you have a rubric or a way to assess your classmates and provide peer feedback?*

9. (If students are watching a video) *Do you have a process to deconstruct the information?* (i.e., a template or chart) *Is it purposeful and is the video tied to your learning?*

We created an acronym, DICE, to help school-based leaders and members of the review team remember to focus on what matters in the classroom.

D—Design of the classroom. Classrooms are learning space. How is the learning made intentional and visible? What are the cuing systems, resources, technology, and desk arrangements? Are there opportunities for interdependent and independent learning?

I—Instructional strategies (or the "how"). How is the teacher transmitting the information? Is it whole class, groups, Q&A? Are the students taking notes from the board or their texts? Are they presenting?

C—Curriculum (or the "what"). If instruction is the "how" then curriculum is the "what." The curriculum concerns the written or formally taught curriculum—outcomes and expectations. Also we suggest you note the complexity: Where does the content fall along Bloom's taxonomy continuum?

E—Engagement. Are the students compliant and attentive or are they actively involved in the task? Are they actually creating new knowledge and engaged? How will you differentiate between compliance and engagement? What are the look-fors? The external review teams should discuss this.

Remember, as you are contemplating reviews, you need to ask the right questions and ensure the right staff are working on the project. Education is about learning from the individual review but also from the collective process. School reviews become value-added when there are explicit links based on the analysis of the results to improved student outcomes. Collectively, we are raising the bar in terms of our expectations for success for all learners and closing gaps for those groups which are underachieving in terms of their potential.

Figure 2.3 provides some questions for you at a system and a school level to consider as part of the policy, process, procedure, and protocol design.

CAPACITY BUILDING

We believe there is a set of skills and knowledge that participants require to effectively plan and implement the collaborative school review policy and process. It's an investment in "cognitive capital" at a school and system level (Costa, Garmston, & Zimmerman, 2012, p. 26). These skills vary in terms of roles and responsibilities but include expertise in the following: facilitation, planning, analysis, classroom observation, collaboration, and teamwork both as a team leader and team member. We refer to these skills as we proceed with the case study. Our model requires that the district conduct a gap analysis and develop a plan for how to build capacity in these areas. Participants both on the school team and the external team need to be trained through a variety of modalities including the use of case studies and scenarios. These should include hands-on experiences. It is important to make the process accessible. According to Hirsh and Hord (2012), "Successful leaders are those who establish regular colleague-based learning teams ... and advocate for the importance of teacher perspective and voice in the decision-making process" (pp. 47–48).

Additionally, the capacity of the organization with regard to material and other supports is critical. The review team needs to assess and provide the necessary resources to ensure reviews can be effectively conducted, and that the suggestions for improvement are built into the organization's day-to-day operation.

Organizational readiness to respond to findings and suggestions for improvement is a key factor in a change process. It is critical to maintain the momentum generated through the review process, as long lags in time to implement erode the momentum, sense of urgency, and commitment developed through the review process. We have seen this thwart improvement and minimize changes brought on by the review process.

There should be a combination of targeted capacity building for the entire system regarding reviews and some "just-in-time" training based on the specific time frames. For example, this may include specific training for schools undergoing reviews in September through December and then

Figure 2.3   Policy, Process, Procedure, and Protocol Considerations for School Reviews

Policy and Design Questions	Design Response	Role/Responsibility	Communication Strategy
What are the expectations for the reviews? What learning or improvement will be measured?			
How will learning and capacity building be embedded in the process?			
Who will make the ongoing decisions during the review process?	Will it be the designated lead, or the reference committee?		
What will be the procedure for selecting schools for reviews?	Will schools volunteer, or will the supervisor select? What will be the cycle of reviews—one year, three years, and five years?		
Who will participate on the system review teams?	Will only administrators participate? Will teachers be included?		
What are the expectations of those participating in the external review team and those at the school being reviewed?			
Will the district direct the orientation process of the review team in the schools being reviewed or leave it to the school's staff to decide on the format?	What are the choices and control available to schools so they can own the process?		

Will there be a verbal debrief at the end of the review day and is it mandatory, open to some staff, or open to all staff?	
What type of dedicated space will be given to the review team on the day of the reviews?	
How much time will each instructional space or classroom observation require?	
Will members of the external team write notes during their classroom observations?	
How will the protocols be clearly communicated?	Will they reside on the district's internal website? Will there be a presentation for board members?
What are the time expectations for when the school can anticipate the written report following their school review and who will present it? How will school staff unpack the written reports?	
How will the system aggregate, disaggregate, and analyze the collective reports?	
How will the system results be publicly reported?	
Who will monitor the school review process?	

training again for schools in the January to March cycle, with a third set of just-in-time training for schools having reviews in the spring term. Training which occurs too early or too late is not as relevant or impactful.

Training and Other Considerations for the Review Teams

It is necessary for schools to ensure that there is a plan to build required capacity. Adult learning will impact student learning. In the design component, describe the capacity required to effectively conduct school reviews and how to identify any gaps that might need to be addressed. There should be common training to build a shared understanding districtwide about the purpose of reviews and their role within a continuous improvement process, as well as the expectations for the review process. Use an adult-friendly learning style (Tate, 2004). This should occur early in the school year and can be based on geographical areas (family of schools) or by panels (elementary, middle schools, and high schools). There needs to be training for both the external review team and the school improvement teams from the schools under review. The just-in-time training should be specific and focused. Part of the training can be combined for the external and internal review teams, and part should be specific to the role.

The agenda for the combined training component could include the following:

- *Protocols and routines required for the collaborative school review—both in written form and a verbal explanation.* Consider if you want these posted on the secure section of your website.
- *Roles, responsibilities, and expectations of team members.* Include these for both the school and the external team.
- *Your data tapestry.* Include the role data or evidence play in the review and discussion and examples of types of evidence that may be used.
- *Classroom observational and analytical skill development.* Provide, in the training, opportunities for data analysis that will parallel the data gathered during an actual review; data collected as well as the student achievement data presented by the school will need to be layered, aggregated, and disaggregated. The protocols for classroom observation have been discussed earlier in this chapter.
- *Experiential opportunities.* Consider using the examples we provide for the Lone Birch pilot schools or create your own simulated reviews or scenarios, or video clips of classroom observations, to give the participants a sense of how the collaborative school review will progress.

- *Time for participants to work in teams.* Allow teams to begin formulating their plans for the onsite visit.
- *Debriefing questions and concerns that may occur during the process.* Use these to revisit the Q&A that can be posted on your intranet.

Staff participation in the planning process matters. Be aware that having school teams participate might result in some supply teacher costs, or this could be done in the afternoon after the school day ends with just refreshments.

For the school-based role specific training, consider asking each school improvement team to bring two pieces of evidence that indicate improved student learning in their building. Have participants in cross-school groupings share the evidence as they explain why they selected these specific pieces. Then they can come back into their own school-based group and discuss the types of evidence other schools consider important. You could also ask the school-based teams to consider five key pieces of information they would want the external review team to know about their school, and why. Three additional ideas for the individual school improvement teams may include sharing their school improvement plans, reviewing what they are thinking of in terms of their presentations, and discussing the flow of the onsite visit so there are no unexpected surprises. A strategy to avoid unexpected surprises is to develop and use in the training some sample timetables based around your school system's timetables.

Review Team Counts Too

During the external review team training, it is important to remind participants of the protocols and issues of confidentiality. They also need experience in examining data and developing findings based on evidence. To assist, consider using the data presented in Chapters 6 and 7 to provide experience in deconstructing classroom observations as a data source; the team can use this to write some beginning analysis based on the data. It is also useful to discuss potential issues that could arise in your district based on its unique context. These discussions could be based on simulations or you might film five- to ten-minute video clips of your own district's classrooms.

ENGAGING STAKEHOLDERS

Based on your own context and culture, determine who needs to be involved. How will they be involved and to what extent? Will decision making occur by consensus? What will be the level of transparency? The team leader should have responsibility for managing the process on a daily basis, but senior management and the system leaders need to understand the process and be seen as knowledgeable and supportive. Think of a success initiative in your current district and try to intentionally parallel this process. School reviews are one component of a broader school improvement effort, so it is essential that their design and the activities related to them be seen by the system as supportive and enhancing rather than duplicating and burdening. The system has to see how reviews fit into the current improvement strategy and cycle. Reviews must not be seen as an add-on or separate and apart from the continuum toward excellence. Alignment can diminish perceived contradictions and bring order out of chaos.

ALIGNING WITH OTHER REQUIREMENTS AND PROCESSES

Effective collaborative school reviews do not exist in isolation. They support and are aligned with other key system improvement initiatives and processes.

Checklist for Aligning Initiatives

Figure 2.4 includes some but not all major common educational initiatives predominant in the literature and practice. Some are big picture, such as establishing clear expectations, and some are more specific, such as using higher-order thinking strategies or implementing balanced literacy and balanced numeracy. You can use this template or create your own matrix to note not only the specific initiative, but also the degree of coherent and embedded practice. You may also highlight your initiatives and then make sure they are embedded in the review so alignment can occur. We cannot stress enough that most school districts and schools are involved in too many initiatives. In change, few are more impactful. The key is to select the right few.

We now return to the Lone Birch School District to see how they are proceeding. In its early days, the initial focus for the leadership team was to conceptualize the design of collaborative school review process. As you read about the discussions occurring at Lone Birch, think of the ways you can integrate the process in your own jurisdiction.

Figure 2.4   List of Possible System Initiatives

System Initiative	Awareness	Some Implementation	Consistent Implementation	Embedded Practice
Establishing clear expectations with SMART goals and gathering student achievement data as evidence				
Implementing Common Core State Standards				
Providing targeted resources based on analysis of the student achievement data				
Designing rich tasks for students to support collaborative problem solving				
Assessment for, as, and of learning, including timely and descriptive feedback				
Implementing research-informed teaching and learning strategies in classrooms such as the Marzano 9 (Marzano, 2003)				
Cocreating or cogenerating exemplars, rubrics, and success criteria to inform the feedback cycle				
Implementing higher-order thinking skills and increasing complexity				
Balanced literacy				

(Continued)

Figure 2.4 (Continued)

System Initiative	Awareness	Some Implementation	Consistent Implementation	Embedded Practice
Balanced math				
Differentiated Instruction and assessment as part of response to intervention (RTI)				
Increasing student voice, leadership, and decision making				
Implementing culturally relevant and responsive curriculum and instruction				
21st-century learning				
Gender-based initiatives				
Restorative discipline programs and problem solving				
Parent engagement and outreach to education stakeholders as partners in the process				
Increased opportunities for homework and practice including peer coaching and homework help via web access				
Responding to ELL through multiliteracies—embedding these in reading and writing texts and strategies and in oracy				

Looking In

Conceptualizing the Collaborative School Review Process

> Policy and design builds the framework of the non-negotiable/closely held. Everything else really concerns the how.
>
> —Lantana Logan, chair of the Lone Birch School District

> I used the upcoming review to galvanize my staff and we collectively looked at what was working, what wasn't. Then we tried to figure out why and where we would go from there.
>
> —Lisa, a superintendent in a neighboring school district

Lea, the superintendent in the Lone Birch School District (LBSD), understands the concepts of effective change management. She knows that a change agenda needs to be contextualized and that action to bring about the change needs to carefully align with other critical and related activities taking place within the system and outside the system. She worries about system fatigue. Lea reflects, "Are there too many directions and initiatives in play?" She understands that administrators suffer from PDD—being pulled in different directions (see Figure 2.5).

Focusing on an effective design ensures that the change process is connected, rationalized, reasonable, and that any changes introduced are sustainable. Lea begins the process by leading her senior team through an examination of the status quo of Lone Birch's change agenda.

Figure 2.5 Pulled in Different Directions (PDD)

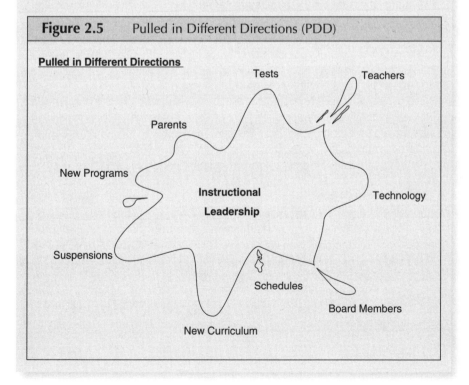

Lea uses the elements of a strategic planning process: a scan of what needs to be taken into account (both the external and internal realities), an assessment of their strengths and the opportunities for changes, a gap analysis, the identification of key strategies, and the establishment of an action plan to achieve those strategies. In her mind, she envisions a cross-departmental team to assist in the design and planning—a strategy that Lone Birch has used before, but she wants the recommendations for how to proceed to emerge from the discussions so that the team will share ownership. Everyone around the table agrees that increasing student achievement, especially in literacy and numeracy, are core at Lone Birch, but is this being reflected in the ongoing work of the schools? The senior team describes itself as data-driven. They have a data tapestry of Lone Birch and use data to set and monitor the targets and goals, but what is the reality at an individual school?

At the initial conceptualization and design meeting, Lea begins: What do we value as a system, and as schools, and why? Lea understands that these values and directions have to align across the district, so that the schools focus on the same goals for the district. The strategies arising from the mission and direction must be complementary and mutually reinforcing. The district's mission is "All Students Achieve." In creating this, senior management and the Lone Birch board members hope that this shared direction on improvement and learning will give Lone Birch a sense of common purpose.

Lea continues to probe in this initial meeting. She asks: What have we done or are we doing in terms of moving the agenda of improvement forward? Lea wants them to think about current and past initiatives in which Lone Birch is engaged: Which ones have been successful? What makes them successful? Lea wants to identify those components that have made past initiatives work and use those components to shape the collaborative school review process: How are we doing? What is our evidence? How do we stack up with where we are and where we want to be?

The senior team thinks about her questions and then discusses the various initiatives currently operating in Lone Birch designed to increased student achievement. They also discuss the range of informed practices undertaken in recent years. They consider issues such as balanced literacy, differentiation, and equitable and inclusionary practices. Balanced literacy is considered a success but what assisted its implementation? Dante—one of the superintendents on the senior team—raises previous implementation issues they faced as Lone Birch rolled out its technology plan. He reminds his colleagues of the challenges experienced during the execution of the new technology plan as the system simultaneously adopted a new platform, new hardware, and new software. The initial result was chaotic until clear systemwide processes and protocols were developed and interdepartmental communication improved. Dante says that these are lessons learned that can be used in developing the proposed collaborative school review process.

Lone Birch is in the third year of their five-year district improvement plan (LBDIP). Lea provides each member of the team with a copy of the LBDIP with its four SMART goals:

1. Increase student achievement in reading and writing and numeracy by 3 percent, as measured on the high-stakes assessments, and close achievement gaps (gender, ELL, special education) by 5 percent.
2. Expand student voice and engagement by 10 percent, as measured in the annual student attitudinal surveys and participation in student councils, cocurricular clubs, teams, and other activities.
3. Increase home/school/community partnerships by 5 percent, as measured by participation in parent councils, attendance of parent/community meetings, parent forums, survey responses, and partnerships developed within the community.
4. Create inclusive, equitable, and inviting learning environments through an increased use of technology and inclusionary practices by 15%, as measured by the continued roll-out of laptops and wireless environments; sessions held on inclusionary practices including the increased use of differentiation, with follow-up teacher self-assessment surveys; decrease in office referrals and suspensions; attendance; parent comments and feedback from students on individual education plans (IEPs); parent and community members' responses on surveys and in focus groups; and input from Lone Birch's special education advisory group (SEAG).

Within each SMART goal are the strategies Lone Birch has also been implementing, such as balanced literacy, differentiated instruction, gender-specific interventions, and assessment for learning to improve student achievement in literacy and numeracy. The senior team understands they need to construct a design for collaborative school reviews that embed their SMART goals and specific practices.

Lea asks them to consider the questions she herself has been considering: Do we have too many initiatives? Are they the right ones? Are the strategies and actions designed to support our SMART goals actually happening in our schools? Lea assures them that "the collaborative school review process will shine light on the evidence and at the end, we will know more than we do now."

Lea, Dante, Juan, Katie, Clay, and Maria understand that the various district initiatives and strategies need to be interconnected. They have looked at the research indicating that improvement in high-performing schools and school districts is coherent and aligned (Leithwood et al., 2009). Dante has shared his reflections of Lone Birch's previous experiences with the technology roll-out and reminds them that beginning a new strategy may impact the implementation of and commitment to other ones. Juan talks about some of the unintended consequences experienced in implementing past strategies such as positive citizenship and stewardship, when preplanning and design were minimal. Katie, one of the supervisors, has been speaking to her colleagues in other districts who are further along in the process.

As senior leaders, they all wonder if the current strategies envisioned in the LBDIP are being implemented effectively across all of the schools. They discuss what they already understand about the collaborative school review process as a possible driver of change and after much discussion, concur that collaborative school reviews might be a useful strategy to help them monitor their SMART goals and focus improvement. Katie, the third superintendent, and Clay, one of the principals, have become the resident experts on a variety of school reviews. Lea knows successful initiatives require champions. They share what they know are the essential conditions necessary for a successful collaborative school review process to occur.

Clay and Katie understand that schools and school systems are only as good as the quality and commitment of the staff that comprise them. The research literature and their own experience has told them that improvement depends on the willingness and ability of administrators and teachers to base their personal practice on effective strategies and best practice. The two know that school and district culture are powerful elements in shifting actual practice and agree that an effective collaborative school review process provides a viable vehicle for engaging systems, for aligning system initiatives, and specifically, for enabling schools and teachers to collectively reflect on how they can achieve greater levels of excellence. It harkens back to the direction from the board members to take Lone Birch from "good to great."

While Lone Birch is unique, it shares many characteristics with other similar school districts. It has pockets of affluence and pockets of poverty, where the economic downturn is impacting families. Lone Birch School District is in fiscal restraint. Although the total student population is declining, some schools are experiencing growth. Lone Birch has an increasing immigrant population with maternal languages other than English. These families are attracted to the cheaper suburban housing and Lone Birch's reputation as a good and safe district. Clay and Katie, with Lea's support, talk about how the design of their process must take into account the unique Lone Birch culture, but more specifically, the climate and reality of the specific schools that would be reviewed. Collaborative school reviews must become a meaningful learning process for staff—one that garners engagement and commitment to doing the review, but more critically, commits to implementing the review's findings. Without this commitment, collaborative reviews become just another fad. Without involving partners in understanding and being able to effectively communicate the purpose, design, and importance, then nothing much might change. The district learned as much from the technology roll-out. It is all agreed, as Lea suggests, this is an opportunity to "know more than we do now" about Lone Birch as a learning organization.

As a team, based on some previous ineffective implementation experiences, they collectively understand the importance of front-loading change. They ask: How do we embed all of this in the design of the process? The departments will work together, they decide. All schools will be involved and the system direction aligned. The senior team thus begins drafting key policy considerations to develop their concept to frame collaborative school reviews.

Lea and her team recognize they need to capture other voices and opinions. Clay is the collaborative school review lead, and he will carry the responsibility until the strategy is implemented and the cycle completed. He will report to Dante, who as a school supervisor serves as the link to senior management and to the various system departments who may be involved. Lea has asked Maria, as a centrally assigned administrator, to assume some of Clay's responsibilities during this process so that no additional salary costs will occur. Lea recognizes that if Clay, as the lead, is pulled off tasks by his normal day-to-day actions, then he cannot spend the dedicated time to ensuring effective reviews occur. Having a designated lead allows for intelligent accountability because someone will be responsible and accountable for monitoring the implementation and is the designate for getting things done.

Assisting Clay as lead is the cross-department reference group mentioned earlier. They are a credible, talented group whose task is to act collaboratively to spearhead the strategy, complete specified tasks, and offer feedback and advice as required. When implementing a system strategy, Lone Birch has used this type of approach before. Senior management envisions that the reference team will function as the operational work team to assist Clay in ensuring that the collaborative school reviews are effectively implemented. The reference team members have a vested interest to succeed and so will look for ways to create collaborative cultures, coalitions, and coherency across the system. Clay, as lead, works with the reference group to maintain the sense of urgency required systemwide. Together they create their terms of reference.

Dante reminds the reference group that questions are a useful way to provoke discussion, share information and perception, and reach consensus on what needs to move forward and what does not. Challenging questions support thinking and improve the process. Dante acknowledges there will be disagreement and challenges, but he and Lea trust the goodwill and the norms in place as part of the Lone Birch culture.[5] The following are questions the committee considers as it begins to design the structure and framework of the Lone Birch collaborative school review process. The members of the reference group are asked questions similar to those Lea had posed to her senior team.

- What do we value as a system (and as schools) and why? In response, Dante and Clay agree it is important that all stakeholders have a shared understanding of the overall mission and vision of Lone Birch.
- How are the aims of the collaborative school review tied to the Lone Birch four SMART goals?
  o Increasing student achievement
  o Expanding student voice and leadership
  o Deepening home/school/community partnerships
  o Creating inclusive, equitable, and inviting learning environments

---

[5] If trust doesn't exist in your jurisdiction take the time, before the process begins, to develop group norms.

- What are the designated and expected outcomes for Lone Birch as a district if the collaborative school review process is successful? If we accomplish the reviews successfully, how will we know—what might be the indicators of success?
- What are the strategies, tools, and resources that we need to accomplish the review goals?
- What are the expectations, and the roles and responsibilities, of the external and internal review team members? From a system or school perspective, what are the barriers and enablers to making reviews happen?
- What resources are required centrally and by the individual schools during the planning and implementation process?
- What are the time lines?
- How will we use the information learned from the collective school reviews to drive change in Lone Birch?
- How will we monitor the process?
- Who will report on its outcomes?

What Happens Next?

To manage the collaborative school review process, the reference team suggests a pilot approach using three representational schools for the first cycle. This way, they can experiment and make sure problems have been worked out before full implementation. The reference group suggests three pilot schools that are representative of Lone Birch in terms of panel, achievement, and sociodemographics. At a systemwide administrator meeting, Lea requests volunteer schools and, remarkably, more administrators volunteer their schools than can be accommodated. Eventually three schools are selected for the initial pilot that are representative of the variation across Lone Birch:

- Pleasant Valley Elementary School—a JK–6 school with 400 students and situated in a lower sociodemographic neighborhood with a high percentage of ELL. Pleasant Valley has shown improvement in terms of the student achievement indicators in the last two years.
- Meadows Middle School—a school with 300 students in Grades 7–8 that is not performing as well as comparable schools in the district. It was once a high-performing school yet students are now struggling and staff is discouraged.
- Harper High School—a school with a student population of over 800 from a traditionally affluent area with a small but growing ELL student population. Harper High is proud of its student achievement record.

Based on the learning from these pilot reviews, revisions will be made to the initial design. The process will be formative, and the results will inform the future process. Lea's mantra is well understood: "Lone Birch is a learning organization."

The reference group frames a strategic communication strategy to inform all stakeholders about the review process and why it is important to school improvement and student achievement. The board members are briefed on the emerging design for the process and notified of the three schools that volunteered. Lea knows that it is essential that board members are kept current. Further communication strategies involve the following:

- All administrators are advised of the collaborative school review strategy at an initial communication session held as part of the regular systemwide administrator meetings. (This is where the solicitation for pilot schools takes place.)
- A message with key points about the review process is posted on the district's website.
- The reference group delivers a presentation to the board members.
- Per request by the reference group, Lea includes information about the reviews in her ongoing blogs to the public.

They are now designing the content and format of the capacity building. The schedule for the mandatory targeted professional learning is being developed for the external review team members as well as the improvement planning teams from each of the three schools.

The reference group, after much deliberation, decides that members of the initial external review teams should be selected based on their expertise and experience. The aim is to develop a pool of reviewers who then can coach and mentor their peers so that as the process progresses, a critical mass of expertise will be available for future reviews and system and school improvement initiatives. Each relevant department is asked to submit a list of names for consideration.

The reference group, with input from the principals' committee, feel that at each individual Lone Birch school, the school improvement team, which had developed the school's improvement plan, will be in charge of the school review planning and preparation. In discussions across several meetings, the reference committee offers suggestions regarding the design. To involve all schools in Lone Birch and to begin the discussions regarding improvement, the reference group makes specific recommendations that include the following:

- A common district self-assessment survey will be used by every school staff member to allow them to reflect on their perceptions of efficacy regarding specific districtwide initiatives focused on learning in their specific campus. The results from the self-assessment survey will form one data set for the individual schools under review.
- The school's supervisor will meet with the designated school-based team in advance of the onsite visit to review the plans.
- The review team will be given some common student achievement data sets in advance of their school visit.[6] The suggested common data are: (1) student population and some demographic characteristics data such as gender, ELL, and students with special needs; (2) suspension/expulsion,

---

[6]If you are not as far along as Lone Birch, use your data to create a tapestry demonstrating achievement in your school or district. This is another example of how context counts.

attendance, and graduation data; (3) assessment scores on the provincial and district assessments; (4) report card data; (5) data from commercially purchased assessments delivered individually or collectively to determine students reading levels, strengths, and areas of need for elementary and middle schools literacy; and (6) for high schools, credit completion data and applications to postsecondary institutions. These data sets already reside in Lone Birch's data management base, are accessible to schools, and will be compiled by the Research Department and made available to the external review teams a week prior to their onsite visit.

- The school staff will determine the content and format of their fifteen- to twenty-minute presentation for the external review team and then decide the additional evidence to share with the review team. Based on the three areas for observation, the school will determine the two areas for focus and the two for feedback.

- All school staff will be invited to an initial meet-and-greet at the beginning of the day of the review to meet the team, and then a closing session at the end of the day to listen to the verbal debrief. Attendance at the verbal debriefing will be voluntary for staff. This aligns with the current operating collective agreements.

- The review team will have a dedicated space for the day and the central office will provide lunch, arranged by the supervisor of the school under review.

- Members of the review team may only use their BlackBerries or smartphones at designated times during the onsite visit.

- All instructional environments in the school will be visited, including the library or resource room, gymnasium, technology labs, computer areas, and arts, music, and drama areas. The exception is the intensive intervention classes, where students with complex mental health issues could become explosive with the addition of new stimuli.

- The school will create a classroom observation timetable for the external review teams, which will be composed of two members.

- The observational visits will be twenty minutes in length, with fifteen minutes of observation in the classroom and five minutes to debrief and get to the next class.

- Clay will write the formal report based on the external review team's collective findings. (Lea had already made the decision that Clay, as the lead, would participate in all three pilot collaborative school reviews.) Within three weeks of the school visit, the supervisor of the school will deliver Clay's formal report to the school's improvement team.

- Funding for release time and resources will be provided to each of the three schools to assist with implementing the suggestions for improvement resulting from the formal report.

- Once all three pilot reports are complete, there will be an analysis of the findings and a presentation to board members regarding collaborative school reviews.

Reader Reflections

When you think about implementing systemwide strategies, what have been your experiences?

When you think of school reviews, what comes to mind? What is your experience with school reviews?

How do you see collaborative school reviews differing from your current practice?

In your district, what might be enablers and barriers for proceeding?

What design features resonate with you and why?

IN SUMMARY

Chapter 1 explained the concept of collaborative school reviews and how these differ from other models of reviews that you may have experienced. This chapter discussed the first characteristic that differs—the way the collaborative school review process is conceptualized within a district improvement framework and how it is subsequently formulated and established. The considerations to be worked include: the tie to other improvement efforts, policy formulation, design of the model, governance, the development of processes and policies, capacity building, stakeholder relationships, and alignment with other requirements and processes.

The establishment of the strategic framework for the use of collaborative school reviews is a key difference. This clearly defines the role of collaborative school reviews within the district's overall improvement strategy and efforts. It links them to other processes and management structures and weaves them into the fabric of the organization. The result is a systemic and disciplined institutionalization of the process across the district.

If you choose to use this model and follow our suggestions laid out in this chapter, you will have systematically thought through the establishment of collaborative school reviews as part of your overall effort to improve teaching practice and student learning. You will have considered how collaborative school reviews, as a process, fit with your improvement strategies and you will have created the structure to support the development, planning, implementation, and monitoring of the process. As a result, you will have in place:

- A policy statement that clearly articulates for the system the value you place on collaborative school reviews, how you plan to use them, and the parameters for their use
- A collaborative school review model and process that has been tailored to meet your context and needs
- A governance structure reflecting the priority you place on this process as a change management strategy
- Procedures and protocols that clearly spell out roles and responsibilities and how the implementation of collaborative school reviews is to be managed
- An understanding of the capacity issues that you will need to address as part of your implementation planning
- Stakeholder understanding of your intentions and aspirations and stakeholder support for the use of collaborative school reviews
- The alignment of the collaborative school review process with the other requirements and processes in your system

For further information and additional resources, please visit the website associated with this book at www.collaborativeschoolreviews.com.

3 Beginning the Planning at the District Level

Spending the time planning helped make the day go so much easier. Sometimes planning is as important as doing.

Lorenzo, a Lone Birch principal

Planning helps me separate the essential from the mundane. What is essential must have priority.

Sedona, a Lone Birch principal

Once the design is in place, what is involved in planning for conducting the school review? How does the planning process begin?

Planning is the tool you use to bring order to the chaos of daily activities and crisis. It should help you anticipate and organize the intended as well as the unintended. For us, planning achieves the following:

- It provides the process for ensuring there is order for the intended and a way of ensuring it occurs according to plan.
- It helps anticipate the unintended and proactively respond when the unexpected might occur.
- It keeps the focus on track and provides a tool for monitoring progress toward achieving your goals.

From the system perspective, as discussed in Chapter 2, the key questions are: What will be non-negotiable and tightly held at the center, applicable to all schools, and what is more discretionary and can be put into the purview of the schools to decide? Planning ensures that the centrally set imperatives and the local discretionary actions happen as intended (see Figure 3.1).

In System Thinking for Curious Managers, Ackoff and Addison (2010) maintained that system thinking requires an understanding of the whole and the parts, and attention to both. They caution that issues arise when the interaction of system parts collide. System thinking requires careful attention to planning. The focus in the second quadrant is the development of a thoughtful and detailed plan of action for implementing the collaborative school review policy. It involves designing a system-level plan as well as detailed school work plans. A system-level capacity-building plan ensures that the intended happens throughout the system and not sporadically within pockets of the system.

System-level efficiencies are an important result of good planning. Think proactively: What planning processes currently operate in your district? Which ones are effective and are working for you? Build your model on those. This way, the planning process for collaborative school reviews will be grounded in the known and aligned to your current directions, realities, and practices. Collaborative school reviews will be, to some extent, challenging because they are both an accountability tool and a mechanism for identifying capacity-building needs. The better the planning involving the interaction of the parts of the system and the more strategic the communication, the fewer challenges you should encounter in implementation (Ackoff & Addison, 2010).

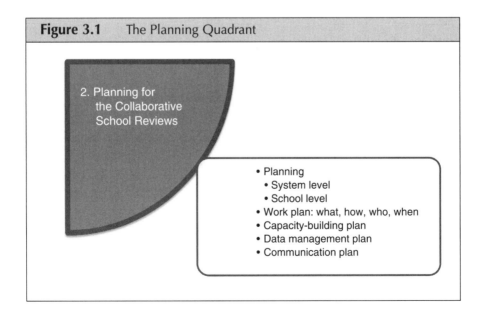

Figure 3.1 The Planning Quadrant

2. Planning for the Collaborative School Reviews

- Planning
  - System level
  - School level
- Work plan: what, how, who, when
- Capacity-building plan
- Data management plan
- Communication plan

Planning at the school and at the system level should take into account the following:

- Activities required to move the collaborative school review strategy forward
- Capacity of the staff involved and how capacity gaps will be addressed
- Data required, and how these data will be collected and interpreted
- How findings will be shared and used
- Management of resources and time lines

We suggest that you document all of these discussions into a detailed work plan that provides a written record of what has been agreed to:

- What will be done? (outcomes)
- How will it be done? (process)
- Who will carry main responsibility? Where will secondary responsibility reside? (governance)
- When will it be done? (time line)

Additionally, the work plan should provide the accountability framework identifying how progress will be monitored, how issues will be identified and addressed, and how results will be reported. This carefully thought-out plan ensures all key players understand and agree to the actions that are to be taken, and accept responsibility for ensuring that they do what is within their power to do to move the plan forward. A collaboratively developed work plan used as a management tool ensures that your organization moves forward in a reasoned and realistic manner with the support it needs to achieve its goals and targets.

Such a plan respects the reality of your organization and the people who work in it. It recognizes their goodwill and their commitment to excellence, but also the limitations and barriers to progress. Such a plan addresses these limitations and barriers and converts them into opportunities for collaboration and joint problem solving.

Districts acting in a systematic way impact student achievement (Marzano & Waters, 2009). The authors from the Mid-continent Research in Education (McREL) argue that districts should encourage, support, and recognize teacher expertise. In *District Leadership That Works*, five responsibilities of district leadership are identified that make a difference:

- *Collaborative goal setting*
- *Non-negotiable goals for instruction*
- *Board alignment in support of district goals*

- *Monitoring goals*
- *Dedicated and aligned resources to support achievement and instructional goals (Marzano & Waters, 2009, p. 6)*

Effective collaborative school reviews can support the execution and monitoring of all five of these responsibilities. Trust is characteristic of high-performing systems. In the absence of trust, Curtis (2011), in *Education Updates,* notes that one finds that there are "imposed short-term targets" and leaders who tend to be "self-protective and micro-manage and are overly directive" (p. 3).

Effective reviews don't just happen. As noted earlier, often the effort and attention has been directed toward short-term implementation of reviews as "flavor of the month" change management efforts. This is something we have learned in Ontario, Canada, with the implementation of the School Effectiveness Framework or SEF (Ontario Ministry of Education, 2010) across 5,000 schools. Good planning is what translates good intention and design into effective action. Effective work plans link action to intended results. Work plans are intentional planning tools. They map out the agreed actions to be taken to achieve the deliverables. They document the accountability structure to measure and track progress. They make explicit key actions that must be taken to achieve the objectives and specify and document the locus of responsibility and established time lines for each action. They clarify outcomes to be achieved and how these will be measured so that the participants will know what progress is being made. The intent is to have everyone on board and moving in the same direction.

As noted earlier, the implementation of collaborative school reviews requires two kinds of work plans: a system level as well as a school level. This chapter addresses the system-level planning process and Chapter 4 covers the school-level planning.

SYSTEM-LEVEL PLANNING PROCESS AND DETAILED WORK PLAN

The system-level plan should be a three- to five-year process that addresses the longer vision for implementing the collaborative school review policy and process. The plan should specify key deliverables, tasks, responsibilities, and time lines. Figure 3.2 provides a draft template for your consideration. The system work plan is a high-level plan that identifies the key implementation steps of the policy and process and intended follow-up.

Figure 3.2 Work Plan Template

Action Required	Role and Designated Responsibility	Cycles & Schools Selected	Time Lines	Resources Required	Data Sets	Capacity Building	Monitoring	Communication/ Reporting	Indicators of Success	Corrective Action

The work plan should provide details about the steps that will occur, including the following:

- Designate the project or team leader, with a focus on knowledge, skills, leadership, and credibility, who will carry the main responsibility for designing, planning, implementing, and monitoring the strategy or goal to a successful conclusion.
- Articulate the specific tasks required, when they are to be taken, what will be monitored, and when completion and results will be reported and to whom.
- Specify indicators of success to measure success and monitor progress.
- Clearly delineate roles, responsibilities, and how each role will be accountable.
- Account for the resources required and dedicated to complete the work plan.
- Outline a communication strategy.
- Include process and time lines for monitoring, which can be in a flowchart format.
- Create forms for reporting on progress and time lines.
- Include a process for taking corrective action including who will be informed and who must be involved.

The collaborative school review teams need to use the work plan as a way to check the status of their work and to ensure that the project is on track and on budget. As the work plan is intended to provide a detailed guide for the orderly implementation of the strategies or initiatives, it should be used to guide the implementation and serve as the basis for securing accountability. The review of the actions completed, along with the gaps between what was intended, what was planned, and what occurred provides an opportunity to regroup and make adjustments to the plan. This is a powerful learning opportunity because it informs the feedback loop to guide future work.

Scheduling the monitoring and reporting activities needs to be included in the work plan. Questions that can be considered in developing the process for monitoring include:

- What were the goals?
- What was planned?
- What were the indicators of success?
- What do the data tell us happened?
- Why did it happen?
- What are the gaps between the intended and the reality?
- What can be done to improve the next time?
- What needs to be changed in the work plan?

CAPACITY-BUILDING PLAN

Teams Matter

Effective work teams are more than just committees. They have clearly articulated goals and each team member has a specified role and responsibility. Effective teams act with intention and focus on achieving agreed-upon results. Working effectively in teams is a 21st-century skill. More and more educators and students require this and specifically for collaboration (Dufour, Dufour, Eaker, & Many, 2010; Grose & Strachan, 2012; Van Clay, Soldwedel, & Many, 2011). Curtis and City (2009) write that the level of team functioning is one predictor of the organization's health. It follows that working together is a core requirement for successful school improvement. You, in your own school and district, will want to make sure that you can assess how you currently function as collaborative teams: Are you collegial or balkanized and territorial? Are your teams productive or do they just endlessly have meetings without resolution? If teamwork is not part of your current culture, you will need to do purposeful team building before you proceed.

Collaboration and open communication have to be mirrored from the top down, from the executive at the district level through to the schools. Dysfunction and mistrust are counterproductive to system improvement; they act as distracters and can prevent staff from supporting and implementing improvement strategies. In fact, Phillips and Hughes (2012) suggest that "the common core means teachers must shift their practice" using "greater teacher collaboration" (p. 32). The collaborative practices required for school reviews can be used to implement new directions such as CCSS or SEF more effectively.

Communication is an important component of the work of teams. Sinek (2009) notes in *Start With Why: How Great Leaders Inspire Everyone to Take Action* that to effectively implement an initiative systemwide, all stakeholders must clearly understand not only what is expected, but more significantly, why it is important for the system and themselves. Transparency and understanding are motivators. Trust must be earned and requires a gradual release of control and sharing of power. The more actively involved stakeholders are in the process, the more ownership occurs. The more teams take ownership, the more their creativity is unleashed and their individual and collective wisdom engaged in achieving the organizational goals.

Collaborative school reviews, as noted previously, are two-tiered—with involvement at both the system and school levels requiring that planning occur simultaneously at both. At the district level, planning requires coordination across the system to enable reviews to happen and to ensure consistent and explicit messages and requirements. Throughout the system, relationships matter. Aligned and effective planning ensures positive relationships and avoids duplication and conflicting priorities. "Being strategic, coherent and well aligned is everyone's business" (Curtis & City, 2009, p. 5).

This chapter explores the planning of those elements that must be tightly held centrally, because these are what the whole system must adhere to, and how these activities might be planned to ensure consistency and compliance. The chapter also addresses how those elements that can be more loosely held are put into the purview of the schools. The elements that need to be included in your own work plan are highlighted once again through our example of Lone Birch as we examine how they are faring.

 **Looking In**

Leadership, Coordination, and Planning at a System Level to Prepare for the Reviews

Clay, the team leader for the collaborative school reviews, has convened a cross-department reference group to enable planning. Maria is assuming some of his normal duties to support the process and minimize costs. The design features, as indicated in the previous chapter, have been set.

The reference committee will set the schedule, ensure all components are planned and ready, and effectively deploy resources to support implementation. Lone Birch has a culture of cross-departments working closely on systemwide projects, so the team knows that establishing a committee that is representative across the system will help address some of the possible issues of balkanization, turf wars, and fragmentation that have arisen with previous initiatives.

Some of the planning issues this reference group discusses include:

- Mechanisms to coordinate departments including Technology, Teaching and Learning, Human Relations (HR), Professional Development, Operations, and Finance
- Scheduling for the three pilot schools' onsite visits and the due date for each of the written reports
- Selecting members for the external review teams
- Scheduling for the capacity-building sessions
- Developing five aligned capacity-building sessions for the external and internal teams, including a discussion of what is effective practice and research-informed learning
- Creating a subgroup to plan and deliver the capacity-building sessions, so that roles, responsibilities, and purpose are shared and understood by all participants
- System provision of funds for release time for capacity building as well as for preparation and implementation of the reviews at a school and system level
- Funds to supply refreshments during the reviews

- Funds for each of the pilot schools to assist with implementing some of the recommendations arising from the review
- Creating a common systemwide self-assessment tool to be administered across all schools prior to the reviews
- Creating a tentative time line to analyze the three completed reports and provide feedback to the system based on the collective analysis

Composition of the External Review Teams

The roles and responsibilities for the external review teams were detailed in the Lone Birch design of their collaborative school review process. It was during the planning phase that members of the initial external review teams were selected based on their expertise and experience. Because Lone Birch was becoming more diverse, and issues of multiliteracies and challenges in accommodating English language learners were a factor, a consultant with that expertise became a member of the external team. Some of the schools had system special education congregated programs, although Lone Birch was a district that supported inclusion so another principal with expertise in special education was also added. There were twenty-five possible members for the external review teams selected across Lone Birch to participate in the first cycle. The three supervisors of the schools (Dante, Juan, and Katie) were included as well as representatives from the administrators' associations. Principals who likely would be experiencing a review in the second cycle were selected as well as the three principals in the first cycle. Coordinating administrators who had responsibilities for safe and secure schools, research, and teaching and learning—including special education, ELL, and French—rounded out the teams. Their expertise will be used where appropriate, based on the school's makeup and focus areas.

Thinking Out

As you consider placement on teams, think about the areas of focus in the district and where that expertise lies. Also, as part of the training for instructional leadership, consider a mix of experienced and less experienced administrators. Remember the process of collaborative school reviews is tied to system learning. The aim is to develop a pool of reviewers who then can coach and mentor their peers so that as the process progresses, a critical mass of expertise develops to support the rest of the organization. This creates real capacity building from within. We maintain that schools must become learning organizations, working together and sharing knowledge across the system.

Looking In

Developing a Self-Assessment Tool

The initial aim at Lone Birch is for the self-assessments to provoke discussions among and between staff on improvement at the school and system levels. The eventual aim is to mirror back the self-assessments and align them with the results of the reviews. This means that Lone Birch needs to achieve the following:

- Create a common tool for self-assessment.
- Coordinate the self-assessment time lines.
- Capture the resulting data and analyze it for patterns and trends.

To achieve these tasks, the reference committee focuses on Lone Birch's current priorities and begins to work on indicators or look-fors at the district, school, classroom, and student levels. Lone Birch previously created a visual measure based on an odometer for the five goals, with a rating scale from awareness through embedded practice (see Figure 3.3). For instance, everyone thought that parent engagement was important, as well as creating safe and inviting learning environments, but what does this actually look like and sound like? What are some indicators?

The Lone Birch Self-Assessment Survey (Figure 3.4) provides an example that you can use to model your own tool.

Data Plan

If Lone Birch student data is to be used effectively, then both the Technology and the Teaching and Learning Departments need to ensure that the appropriate student achievement data can be accessed prior to beginning the cycle of pilot reviews. This entails a discussion of how to effectively use the current data management, collection, and analysis functions within

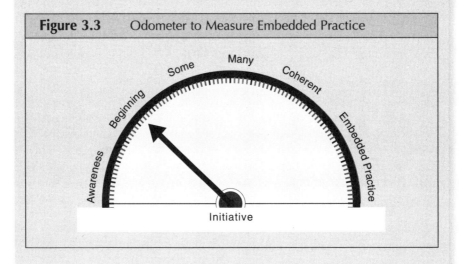

Figure 3.3   Odometer to Measure Embedded Practice

Figure 3.4 Lone Birch Self-Assessment Survey

Category	Level 1: Awareness	Level 2: Beginning	Level 3: Some	Level 4: Many	Level 5: Coherent	Level 6: Embedded Practice
There are high expectations for student achievement.						
Structures, resources, and practices are in place to support student achievement in literacy.						
Structures, resources, and practices are in place to support student achievement in numeracy.						
Targeted evidence-based strategies are in place to affect achievement.						
A variety of assessment data are used to monitor student achievement and inform the next steps in the learning process.						
Interventions for students are timely and tiered and based on evidence.						
Professional learning is job-embedded, data-driven, and focused on increasing capacity in assessment and evaluation.						
Multiple opportunities exist to involve students and to develop and support student leadership and student voice.						

(Continued)

Figure 3.4 (Continued)

Category	Level 1: Awareness	Level 2: Beginning	Level 3: Some	Level 4: Many	Level 5: Coherent	Level 6: Embedded Practice
Parents and community are valued and participate as partners in the learning process.						
Policies and structures are in place to support the school as a safe and secure environment.						
Learning environments are inclusive, reflecting students' unique needs, backgrounds, strengths, and interests.						
Instruction and assessment are differentiated to meet students' needs.						

Level 1—Awareness. PD, reading, and discussion are being implemented by few staff.

Level 2—Beginning implementation. Focus of the staff is on exploring how the initiatives might be implemented and a few staff are beginning to apply.

Level 3—Some implementation. Some staff have begun to implement; likely this will occur within a division or department in a more consistent manner. There might be the beginnings of a professional learning team drilling down on this practice.

Level 4—Many staff implement. Implementation is at a schoolwide level with clearly established purpose, and shared beliefs. There is evidence of collaborative learning among staff and shared practice in classrooms.

Level 5—Coherent practice. There is evidence of ongoing processes in place across the school. There is ongoing moderated practice and evidence of impacts in classrooms.

Level 6—Embedded practice. Practice has become institutionalized schoolwide. The practices are embedded and ongoing. Staff is involved in collaborative inquiry, including data gathering.

Lone Birch—Nelson, the district's technology lead, coordinates with Clay on this. Accessing and analyzing relevant data requires HR and Operations to coordinate the calendars, planning schedules, and time lines to ensure that contractual obligations are followed and that the planning is feasible.

The reference committee, with input from the principals' council, then agrees that each school will select areas for focus that impact student achievement and evidence to support their choices. Two of the areas will reflect strategies or goals that the school feels confident about; two will reflect areas where the school wants feedback, where the school feels it is still in the initial stages of implementation.

Capacity-Building Plan

To address capacity building, Clay assists by placing Maria in charge of the planning. He works with Juan, Dante, Annie, Katie, and the Lone Birch principals' council to make sure that the messaging and materials used in the professional learning sessions provide the necessary skills and knowledge to allow the reviews to proceed.

The reference group decides they need five system-level capacity-building sessions to prepare everyone and provide for common messaging and differentiation in their specific roles and responsibilities. Because no new money is available, they reallocate funds from the existing system professional learning budget. A subgroup takes on designing and delivering these targeted professional learning sessions.

Session 1

Lea and Clay lead this initial session for Dante, Juan, and Katie as more of a guided conversation. As critical leaders in the accountability and improvement process, it is essential that they, as school supervisors, understand their role and the relevant time lines, processes, and indicators. Lea and the rest of senior management recognize that if this group is not aligned and committed to the process, it may adversely affect the review process. These supervisors of schools are both critical friends and active participants. They are responsible for holding the initial meetings at the schools, providing leadership to the external review teams, presenting the verbal feedback, and providing the formal report back to the school's improvement team. Clay, as team leader, will participate in all of the reviews and write the three initial reviews to ensure a common format and coherency across the reviews. The long-range plan is to build capacity across a targeted district review team, composed of representatives from each school team. This team will write the reviews.

As a group, the supervisors review the work plan to monitor progress to date. They look at the draft materials provided and make some suggestions. They talk about enablers and barriers at a school level and try to anticipate possible areas for tension and conflict. It is important that senior management be conversant with the process and that they have an opportunity to work out any issues or concerns they might have about the process. Collectively, Dante, Juan, and Katie—as the school supervisors and leaders of the review team—agree, during their initial meeting with the pilot school administrators and school improvement teams, to ask the following questions within a guided conversational framework:[1]

- Where are you in terms of implementing your current school improvement plan?
- Who will serve on the school's self-improvement team for the collaborative school reviews? How and why were they selected?
- How did staff participate in the self-assessment process?
- How were the data analyzed and collated? What patterns emerged?
- What has been shared with staff regarding the upcoming collaborative school reviews?
- What are your areas for focus and feedback and how were they selected?
- What data or evidence will support the areas for focus and feedback? Why?
- Describe the process that is emerging for preparing for the onsite visit.
- Is there anything we need to know about the upcoming collaborative school reviews here?
- How can we be helpful?

Session 2

Lea and her team lead this session for all school and system administrators to inform them on why Lone Birch has committed to reviews and how reviews can support system and school improvement. This is a regular system meeting focused on school reviews and eventually all schools will participate. The sessions for all principals begin with key messages from Lea and her vision for the reviews. Her presence indicates that this strategy is important.

Participants receive handouts outlining the supporting research, protocols, time lines, templates, and other decisions already made. These materials were prepared well in advance and have been revised and polished based on feedback from the reference group. As with past LBSD initiatives, this is treated as a work in progress. The materials are also placed on the Lone Birch secure intranet site. Clay, as team lead, presents the materials and clarifies any ambiguities. After Clay's introduction, Alessia, a superintendent from a neighboring district who has experience with reviews, talks about their role in improvement and her experiences with the process; she also engages the teams in an open-ended discussion.

A critical piece of this training is the role data or evidence can play in the process. This is where the presenters share the research and best practices.

Self-Assessment Survey

The reference group has created a self-assessment survey tool for Lone Birch (see Figure 3.4). To present and administer the survey, some schools use their

---

[1]In your school or district, use these questions as a model to frame your discussions.

improvement planning teams, others establish a new committee, and still others use the existing structure of department heads. The "how" is the responsibility of each school; however, the survey tool is to be common across schools.

The process of engaging staff in the self-assessment survey should allow administrators an opportunity to talk about school improvement. It should also give staff an opportunity to identify where they perceive their school in terms of key goals, with resulting discussions including where they should be. These discussions will form a regular school staff meeting, so there are no additional charges. In advance of the formal reviews, the aim is that Lone Birch school staff will be individually and collectively involved in improvement and build ownership and share understanding. Schools will have one month to administer the survey and send their results to Clay. The survey results will then be aggregated and analyzed to begin to establish some baseline data for Lone Birch as a system.

Session 3

Clay leads the third session, which is just for the three principals of the pilot schools. This meeting is to make sure the principals understand all of the processes and components required, and the role that each of them will play in orchestrating the reviews in their own schools. Lea and Clay review the key features for Lone Birch's design. The dates for each school's onsite visit are set to occur within three months of this meeting. This doesn't give the three pilot schools a lot of time to prepare, but the design frame for the reviews is complete and the planning process has begun. They also set dates for capacity building for central training for the three school improvement planning teams and select members for the external review team. Planning at the school level can thus begin in earnest.

After discussion with the superintendent and their three supervisors, the three pilot principals agree on a common planning format with cascading events:

- The three pilot principals will meet with their individual school improvement planning team and their respective school supervisor. The questions the supervisor will use are referenced earlier in this chapter.
- Each pilot school will hold a meeting with all staff to brief them about the review process, including the onsite visit and relevant time lines. The supervisor of the school will attend that meeting and answer any other questions to ensure the process is unfolding according to the plan.
- The three school improvement teams will attend the specialized training designed for the three schools involved in the pilot reviews.

It is decided that the improvement team, led by the principal, will meet with their supervisors prior to the initial staff meeting, then one month before the review, and then two weeks before the review to ensure everything is on schedule.

Resources for Sessions 4 and 5

To assist in the more specific training for the external review team and the school improvement teams, the Lone Birch subcommittee of the reference group creates a fictional junior high school with relevant student achievement data. The use of simulations and data from a fictional school allows participants to experience the analysis process that will be used during their own review and provides a vehicle and content for all three schools to consider. The aim is to engage participants in a review simulation in order to identify some questions and possible trends and patterns in the data. A PowerPoint embeds video clips of actual Lone Birch classrooms, simulating what the review teams may observe during the onsite visit. The Teaching and Learning Department also develops look-fors or indicators for the school improvement teams and the external review teams. The reference team, with system input, creates an evidence summary template that can be used in the training sessions (see Figure 3.5). The school's improvement team then works with staff to complete the template for their individual school, gather the evidence they want to share, and prepare the presentation.

Session 4

Clay leads the fourth session, for the three school-based administrators and their school improvement teams, to drill down the expectations and protocols for the actual review. This school-specific training examines the protocols, process, and roles for members of the review team. In particular, it emphasizes the role of evidence. School-based data and video clips simulate a review so each participant understands the role of the external review. They also review the non-negotiables and discuss options for how schools can individualize their reviews. They discuss what types of evidence they might present to the external review team for their onsite visit and what their presentations to the review team could entail. Clay also introduces the evidence summary template. Many good ideas arise, but no final decisions are reached because everything must first go back to the individual school staff for input.

Reader Reflections

As you plan for implementation, sometimes components of the proposed plan need to be reworked. We offer you choices, and your district can select common areas of focus to emphasize alignment or the schools can select their own area of focus or have a combination of each. All demand thoughtful discussions and the gathering of evidence. If there is already a fair degree of alignment, you may want to select common areas of focus and if there is a wider variety among and between schools, initially you may want to ask each school to self-identify the areas of focus for the reviews. These areas should be strategies or initiatives that impact student achievement and are aligned with the district plan.

Of all of the initiatives in your district, which have the greatest effect on student achievement? How do you know? What is your evidence?

Figure 3.5	Evidence Summary Template				
Area of Focus	Rationale for the Selected Area of Focus	Evidence in the School Improvement Plan	Evidence in Classrooms in Terms of Student Learning	Evidence in Public Spaces of the School (halls, offices, library, and other public spaces) and in Messaging to the Parents and Community	Additional Comments & Information
Focus Area 1					
Focus Area 2					
Focus Area for Feedback 1					
Focus Area for Feedback 2					

Session 5

Clay again leads the fifth and final training session for those twenty-five members of Lone Birch selected to serve on the three external review teams. This training describes the protocols, process, routines, and non-negotiable for members of the external review team. It, like Session 4, also emphasizes the role of evidence. School-based data and video clips again simulate a review so they can better understand their roles. There are scenarios of draft verbal and written reviews presented so that the members of the external review teams can provide their input. The school-based and external review team session mirror one another, but speak to the specific roles and responsibilities each will face. Sessions 4 and 5 use complementary materials.

District central staff talk about how they can support the schools during the review process, including providing materials and release time for planning. They also conduct some heated discussion regarding the use of data as a source of evidence: What should the external reviews team members be looking at and why? Does the simulated evidence confirm the areas of focus and the evidence summary?

In their session, the external review members work through their observations of the videotaped classrooms in pairs and discuss what they observe relative to the simulated review. Members talk about the data and observations and based on this, what might be some areas they can address in their upcoming collaborative school review.

Following the sessions and relying on input from the participants in Sessions 4 and 5, Clay decides to use a variance of the template featured in Figure 3.6 to take notes during the actual school visits, as per Figure 3.7.

With the training complete and the templates now customized, the three improvement teams and the members of the external review teams are ready. The focus for Lone Birch moved from the center to the individual schools and the next phase of planning commences, with the process well underway. Discussion at both levels focused on data and evidence. The buzz has begun and people in the district are talking about the upcoming collaborative school reviews.

Figure 3.6	Onsite Data Gathering Template			
Area of Focus	Evidence From the Presentation	Observational Evidence in Classrooms in Terms of Student Learning	Evidence in Public Spaces of the School (halls, offices, library, and other public spaces) and in Messaging to the Parents and Community	Suggested Next Steps
Focus Area 1				
Focus Area 2				
Focus Area for Feedback 1				
Focus Area for Feedback 2				
Three suggestions for the school improvement plan 1. 2. 3.				

Thinking Out

We gather and analyze data so that we understand where we are and where we have to be. The data can create a visual of student achievement in a school or district—its strengths and challenges. Data may not provide the answers, but they will raise the questions you need to ask to improve.

DATA MANAGEMENT PLAN: CREATING A DATA TAPESTRY

How are we accountable? We think of data as evidence. Bernhardt (2004) argues that schools and school systems that gather data but often do not systematically aggregate them, disaggregate them, analyze them, or use them to inform practice are less effective with impacting achievement than school systems that do. Data, according to Bernhardt (2004), can assist schools and school systems achieve the following:

- Identify achievement gaps and then specify some gap areas to raise the academic bar between where the school currently is and where it wants to be (SMART goals in the improvement plans—strategic, measureable, attainable, and time-driven).
- Move from what one American superintendent once referred to as "cardiac evidence"—moving from perception, "we believe this is where we are as a district," to using facts and evidence to demonstrate where change is really required and to measure the effects of interventions as they are implemented.
- Demonstrate whether and to what extent the SMART goals are realized at the school and system level.
- Assess collective strengths and needs of staff and students.
- Identify possible and probable root causes for the achievement gaps to assist in becoming less reactive and more proactive.
- Use the research and effective practices that align with the identified gaps and possible or probable root causes.
- Review the current funding of resources and strategies at a district level to align with closing the gaps and raising bars.
- Inform the professional learning that needs to occur to build capacity to reach the goals and targets.
- Provide data to review ineffective practices.

- Allow the schools to use evidence and feedback to review and revise their plans for improvement in the continuum of improvement.
- Begin the cycle again—it is all about continuous improvement to improve student learning.

We use the data to create a tapestry so that school staff have a better sense of what is working and what is not, and most important, why or why not. Then these schools can provide a sustained focus on improvement of student achievement over time. An efficient and effective data management system provides schools with relevant information regarding their performance. Collaborative school reviews reflect back by referencing and aligning existing achievement data sets. They indicate levels of coherency of practice with regard to the initiatives the school has selected.

An effective and efficient data management system provides thoughtful use of evidence and thus assists schools in establishing direction, benchmarks, and indicators of success. Accessing and using multiple measures of student achievement data helps in creating the tapestry to drill down and identify what is working and what is not, and for which students. It allows schools to measure progress over time and shape targeted strategies for improvement. The four-quadrant framework requires data in each of the design, planning, implementation, and accountability quadrants. Given the global accountability agenda, schools and school systems are responsible for publically demonstrating improvement. The targets and indicators of achievement—whether national, state, or provincial assessments; graduation rates; retention rates; course completions; suspension data; or attitudinal survey data—are part of the tapestry for intelligent accountability. The education community's progress in moving toward measureable targets using specific indicators builds public confidence. We are publicly accountable for improvement.

Districts produce many differing forms of data linked to student achievement. As mentioned earlier, efficient and effective data management systems are a component of most high-performing districts. Most now have provisions for gathering data centrally. Effective districts not only aggregate data but also disaggregate into subgroups and analyze data to identify trends and patterns. This requires a data management system, as schools must work with the data to overlay data sets, aggregate, disaggregate, and then communicate or present it in dynamic ways. Staff require a system like this in order to see patterns and trends, make sense of the data, and begin to use effective strategies to impact learning. As you proceed toward collaborative school reviews, examine the current state of your data management system: Where does responsibility for data management reside? Are the data refreshed or static? Can schools access the data required to improve? Can the current data management system produce a synopsis of the data that the external teams can use? What are the capacities of school-based staff and system-level staff in terms of data literacy? What are the data sets you as a district or school are currently managing? Figure 3.7 provides a chart of possible or likely data sets for use in your planning.

Figure 3.7	Possible Data Sets		
Data Set	**Time Lines**	**Panel/Grade/ School Where Used**	**Details**
Sociodemographic			
Enrollment—total student population of the school			
Enrollment by grade/subject			
Gender			
Maternal language(s)			
Number of students requiring special education services and programs			
Culture/race			
Student Learning			
Student achievement data by subject/grade			
Standardized tests or standards-based tests			
Norm-referenced tests			
Criterion-referenced tests			
District-designed tests			
Authentic assessments			

(Continued)

Figure 3.7	(Continued)		
Data Set	Time Lines	Panel/Grade/ School Where Used	Details
Credit rescue & recovery for high school students			
Observational data			
Report card			
Graduation rates			
Application to postsecondary institutions			
Attendance			
Suspension/ expulsion			
Perceptual			
Climate surveys			
Attitudinal data surveys			

It is important to consider whether the data you have are relevant, verifiable, accurate, and reliable. Are the data generally accepted as valid measures of success? The more data-rich and data-literate a system is, the easier the process of selecting evidence becomes. These are the conversations necessary for improvement. In probing for answers, the system can learn. Effective systems use data as metrics to establish where they are, where they have been, and what needs to happen to realize their key goals. Collaborative school reviews measure accountability through performance.

Most likely, you are already gathering many of these. Figure 3.7 includes others for your consideration. Perceptual data are another important source although less frequently used. Do you know how students feel about their learning? Which subjects do students like the best? With which subjects do they feel more effective as learners? How do parents rate their sense of engagement as members of the school community? How do staff view their efforts to improve student learning? The self-assessment data are perceptual data. If you are looking for other types of self-assessment, Van Clay, Soldwedel, and Many (2011), in *School Self-Assessment,* include self-assessment forms. The effective schools literature includes correlates that can be used as the basis for self-assessment.

Observational data, gained from being purposely visible in schools, in hallways, and most important in classrooms, are yet another source of data to be probed during the review process. You will want to include these in the structure and flow of the review. We have dealt with classroom observations at length in the previous chapter and given you questions and protocols as a model.

Of all the data sets, what will be the most useful and impactful for a collaborative school review? Which will create a data tapestry? Again, Figure 3.7 provides a tool for use when your system is considering the issue of data and what types of data to include as part of your collaborative school review process.

 Looking In ────────────────────────────────

Lone Birch's Data Management Plan

At Lone Birch, the reference group now discusses the issue of data. Which data sets could and should inform the reviews? What will be centrally created and what will be in the purview of the schools to select, collate, and present? They agree that system data will be prepared and given to the external review team in advance of the review. For this, the Technology Department partners with Teaching and Learning to gather and provide the data in a package for the school improvement teams and the external review teams. These two departments agree that the data package will include:

For all schools,

- Deconstructed high-stakes assessment results
- Some sociodemographic data for each school—total number of students, gender, the number and percentage of students with maternal languages other than English (ELL), and the percentage of students with special education needs based on their panel

For elementary schools,

- Enrollment
- Student success data by subject and grade, and a synopsis by grade of their report card data
- Data gathered to determine students' reading and writing levels, and other literacy measures data or appropriate literacy data
- Discipline data (suspensions, expulsions)
- Student and parent climate survey data

For secondary schools,

- Enrollment
- Student success by subject and grade

- Credit completion data
- Credit rescue and recovery data
- Graduation data
- Attitudinal survey data and the percentage of students applying to post-secondary institutions (university, community, and technological colleges)

The reference group decides that the schools will use the focus areas aligned to the district improvement plan (as outlined in the self-assessment survey) to identify the evidence to demonstrate what is working well in terms of their school improvement plans and what areas they want feedback on. Each pilot school will select two areas for focus and two for feedback. Schools can provide additional data sets as part of the package prepared for the external teams to consider, such as running records or their own student survey data, or parental survey data if that is something they already have.[2]

Thinking Out

In our experiences, the types and presentation of school-selected evidence can vary widely and this should be within their purview, as long as the system data are part of the package for the collaborative school reviews. We have reviewed posters with student achievement data, agendas of professional learning team and faculty meetings, agendas from capacity-building sessions, pictures, copies of any previous reports, teacher blogs and websites, and binders. These are all useful sources and provide insights into what is valued at the school, that is, what is actually going on. One caution is to allow for additional time during the planning phase to take into account a plethora or surfeit of data. Members from the external review team will need time built into the schedule to examine all the data presented. In the training, you need to pay particular attention to the review team's ability to understand data sets as well as the system's ability to select and present data so that the meanings can be easily understood. Consider a session of data literacy for the review teams, because this is an area of capacity building that most systems lack and improvement would be useful.

COMMUNICATION PLAN

In a model where the responsibility for data is shared, "accountability must be a reciprocal process" (Furhman & Elmore, 2004, p. 294). All members

---

[2]For Lone Birch, this was data they are already gathering. For your district/school, you may be at a different place along the continuum. Work with the data you have and begin to plan for the data you need to create a tapestry.

of the school and system must become responsible for improvement. Lone Birch demonstrates a balance of tight and loose leadership. The district, by mandating that the central gathering of data is supplemented by school-based data, put a focus on the use of evidence. This in turn supported the emergence of conversations in schools and at a system level concerning the effectiveness of the current assessment or accountability system. Collaborative school reviews can shine a spotlight on the effectiveness and purpose of summative and formative data that are gathered and provide an opportunity for a system to become more data-literate. In the monitoring of the collaborative school reviews and deconstruction of the process, districts like Lone Birch can see where they are and how they can ensure a balanced and coherent system of assessment that can drive classroom learning.

Communication and Engagement

In his book, *Drive: The Surprising Truth About What Motivates Us,* Daniel Pink (2009) shed light on research that demonstrates individuals are more willing to dedicate time and energy to a project if they find some personal connection to the task at hand. School reviews enable teachers to reflect on the holistic and pedagogical aspects of education in their own school and enhance their connection to their school and to improvement (Harris et al., 2003).

Remember our advice regarding teams and effective teamwork; the same applies to strategic communication: Who has to be engaged and who has to be involved in the process? What are the key messages? The nonnegotiable is that the system leaders need to understand, support, and clearly explain the intent, the rationale, the process, and the desired outcomes for collaborative school reviews. The school leaders must also understand, support, and engage their staff in the process of collaborative school reviews. Staff that lead or participate in the external review teams require an in-depth understanding of the policy, the model, the process, and the protocols. They have to know what is expected and to be absolutely clear about the parameters and protocols for their roles. They must understand the desired final outcomes and the requirements for the verbal and written reports and they must be able to deliver these.

The direction of the strategic communication plan has to be for transparency and common messaging. It needs to emphasize the key goals for the collaborative school reviews. It has to communicate the importance of using data as evidence to inform the school improvement process or DIDM—data-informed decision making.

Remember that if there are no clear messages or agreement on the processes and protocols, then there is a greater chance for ambiguity and for individuals to discern their own biased messages and transmit these to staff. Consistency in design and planning helps achieve intentionality and coherency and greater adherence to intent and purpose. Too many district and school reviews suffer from messaging that is fragmented and open to individual interpretation. These become barriers to improvement.

Communication Components

Communicating the policy, design, and process to follow for the collaborative school reviews is a multifaceted process that involves a number of considerations and activities. We suggest that you take time in the planning process to think it through and to document what you will do, how, and when. You will want to consider the following:

- The objective for your communication strategy
- The key messages that you need to deliver
- Who needs to be reached
- The potential issues and concerns that may arise
- Ways that you can position your message to get your intent understood
- The forums, formats, and materials that you need to produce
- Time lines and responsibilities for moving forward

Figure 3.8 provides a template for a communication plan.

Figure 3.8   Communications Plan Outline
Objective of the plan:
Key messages to be delivered:
Target audiences:
Senior administration/executive officers
Corporate staff
Principals
Teachers
School staff
Board members
Chair of the board

Situational Analysis:

Potential issues and concerns

Positioning of messages:

Communications strategy:

Key activities

Tools and materials

Responsibilities:

Director

Executive officers

Supervisory officers

Collaborative school review lead

Reference groups, etc.

External review team

Principals

School review team

Summary of Promotional Materials to Be Produced				
Target Audience	Activity/ Product	Timing	Responsibility	Estimated Cost

Looking In

Other Planning Considerations for Lone Birch

In talking with other districts about the structure of the review process, Clay and Dante remember some other planning considerations. They broach this list with the reference group and collectively agree on the following:

- The external review team will require dedicated space for confidential discussions during the school visit. Schools would be asked to provide this.
- Clay will bring his laptop with a secure memory key to all onsite visits. The individual schools will be asked to provide a SMART Board or data projector so that preliminary findings can be shared across the external team. This way all members of the external team will cocreate the findings.
- Lunch will be provided for the external review team. Discussion ranges back and forth on this, especially in a time of fiscal restraints, yet providing lunch for the external team enables working lunches and makes the team's work more effective. The members of the reference team are clear that it cannot be that on one review, lunch is provided but on others it is not. Funds would thus be provided centrally. While the allocation of funds for the reviews in a time of fiscal restraints means that another initiative is dropped or stalled, the reference group knows that it is all about strategic choices of where to put time, money, and effort. Collaborative school reviews provide one such strategic choice.

Reader Reflections

Researchers recognize the importance of the impact of reflection on teacher learning (Harris et al., 2003). We work in reactive climates. There are immediate demands on our time and issues that require resolution, now. If the review process is to be effective, spend the time front-loading. Plan. This process worked out contextually for Lone Birch. In your district, another process might be better suited.

What are the taken-for-granted assumptions about people and processes in your district?

What is the situation regarding aligned messaging in your jurisdiction and what is the evidence you would use to justify your answer?

In your district, what design and planning has already occurred?

What are your key district messages?

If staff were polled, would their responses on key messages match yours? Why or why not?

We are now ready to zero in on how the three schools are planning for the reviews in the next chapter. The system design and planning is complete.

IN SUMMARY

Another key difference between collaborative school reviews and other school review models is a focus on design and planning prior to implementation. We believe that a carefully thought-out approach is a prerequisite. The value of the school reviews will be greatly determined by careful attention paid to planning the reviews and the capacity building to conduct them. This ensures that the system is able to conduct the reviews in a manner to truly derive the benefits. The planning includes both a district-level plan and plans at the school level. This chapter has discussed the development of the district-level plan and what that should entail. This includes a work plan, a capacity-building plan, a data management plan, and a communication plan. In working through the planning cycle you will have included the following:

- *In a structured work plan, detailing key actions that you will take to implement the collaborative school review process.* This includes what you will be doing, how you will be doing it, who will be involved and responsible, and the time lines.
- *Identifying the capacity that you will need to implement the collaborative school review process and the gaps that you will need to address.* You will have determined the best way to address those gaps and have developed a plan for moving forward. This includes an overall strategy and tactics.
- *Identifying the data that you will need to implement the collaborative school review process and any issues related to their access.* You will have developed a data management plan that ensures that you will have access to the data and their analysis to support the effective implementation of the process.
- *Developing a communication plan.* This will inform and engage staff and stakeholders in implementing the process.

For further information and additional resources, please visit the website associated with this book at www.collaborativeschoolreviews.com.

4 Continuing Planning at the School Level

Lesleigh Dye (2012), superintendent of schools for the Rainbow District School Board in Sudbury, Ontario, Canada, feels that school reviews are a process "that enables superintendents and school staff to focus on specific instruction strategies that make a difference for students. It is a wonderful opportunity for schools to showcase their successes and hear considerations for next steps."

Planning for the review at the school level is as critical as the planning at the district level. What differentiates this more localized planning is the understanding that, if student improvement is to occur, this is where the real change needs to happen. Thus it is essential that the school staff be engaged, that they buy in, and that they become active contributors to the process. Their input needs to shape the way forward. Without shared planning and engagement at the school level, collaborative school reviews are just another centrally mandated process. This chapter uses the three pilot schools to demonstrate preparation at the school level. You can use the process described in this chapter, whether or not you and your district elect to include a pilot component as part of the design process.

The previous chapters discussed those areas that need to be tightly held at the system level. This chapter begins to describe those areas that the system may have already established as a non-negotiable for collaborative school reviews, as well as those areas that may have been determined as loosely held, discretionary, and placed in the schools' purview.

Figure 4.1 provides a template for your consideration as you develop the action plan for your schools. It can help organize the planning process and provide a checklist to make sure you cover all the items that need to be planned.

Figure 4.1	School Action Planning Template			
Task	**Responsibility**	**Resources/ Costs (human, room allocation, technology, refreshments, etc.)**	**Time Lines**	**Additional Notes**
Selecting the areas for priority and feedback				
Gathering the data/evidence				
Preparing the packages for the external review team				
Organizing the evidence				
Logistics & planning requirements				
Key messaging for staff				
Presentation for external review team				
Debriefing				
Public communication				

LAYERING THE SCHOOL-BASED PRIORITIES ON THE DISTRICT PRIORITIES

As educational systems, our core aim is to collectively increase student achievement for all students. Chapters 2 and 3 explained how to establish system priorities to frame the collaborative school review process. The initial discussion at the school level begins with developing the key system goals. Layering the school-based priorities on the district priorities ensures both alignment to the district and inclusion of local context. The process of identifying these goals to frame the review process at the school level will involve planful discussion and requires facilitation skills. Schools need to begin planning for the collaborative school review as soon as possible to effectively address all the data needs and logistics.

Recognize that the process will be challenging but remember that it is a valuable journey that will yield many positive results. It will take time to clarify and build collaboration and shared understanding among the stakeholders so that agreements can be reached about how to best proceed. Once overall agreement is reached, planning activity needs to focus on generating the evidence that will be used at each school.

There are some key questions driving the development of the evidence summary at a school level. These form the framework for schools when they prepare their evidence summary template. The reference team lead by Clay wants the schools to think about the following:

- What do we already know about student achievement in our school?
- What are two areas of strength (for focus) and two we are still challenged by (for feedback)?
- What are the trends in terms of learning needs?
- What strategies, actions, and interventions are in place?
- What are we considering based on our analysis?
- What professional learning is supporting these strategies, actions, and interventions?
- What is our evidence at a school and classroom level?

The school's improvement team works with staff to complete the template for their individual school, gather the evidence they want to share, and prepare the presentation for the external review team (refer back to Figure 3.5 in Chapter 3). As their planning commences, they will meet with their respective school supervisor.

Pleasant Valley

There is a buzz in the halls of Pleasant Valley Elementary School. Under Jill's leadership, the staff is excited about the upcoming review. During her four years at Pleasant Valley, Jill has built a culture of trust and the teachers respect her expertise in terms of literacy and professional learning. The school has changed from a place where behavior issues and low academic achievement was the norm to one where respect and hope now dominate. Jill and her team have reached out to the community and begun to bring the school into the homes of students. With parental and student input, they developed a code of behavior. Teachers collectively began to implement effective class routines and with their individual classes coconstructed classroom norms that were posted in every classroom. An early literacy program, under Jill's leadership, was also implemented and several times a year, parents or caregivers are invited into the library with their preschoolers for open reading sessions to provide some reading readiness.

As a result of Jill's leadership, staff work in learning teams. One of the learning teams focuses on differentiation of instruction and assessment and continues to share its growing expertise with the other staff, another works on problem solving and communication in math, and a third on guided reading and questions leading to accountable talk. "Learning Together" has become Pleasant Valley's motto. From the beginning, Jill had a clear idea of her purpose as an instructional leader; coming from the central office as a literacy coach, she had skills and experiences in the areas that were important to Pleasant Valley. Historically, the school faced challenges in terms of behavior issues and academic achievement; they had high student suspension rates and low scores on high-stakes assessments and on many of the other indicators. There had also been a high staff turnover. When Jill came to Pleasant Valley, it wasn't a school of choice for staff or for parents and their children. Most students came from lower socioeconomic backgrounds and their parents worked in part-time and often transient jobs. Staff had blamed parents for a perceived lack of interest. Homework wasn't done, literacy scores were low, and parental meetings were not well-attended. Jill believed that changing staff behaviors and practices would change students' behaviors and achievement. She worked hard to convince staff that lack of improvement wasn't a blame game, but a real opportunity. She shared the very real evidence that students facing challenging circumstances can succeed and excel if teaching and learning become focused, intentional, and coherent using evidence-informed practices.

Jill has a quote from the book *Creating the Dynamic Classroom* posted above her desk,

> With so much to consider, it can be a daunting task for teachers to create an effective program that addresses the multiple literacies of today and tomorrow, while at the same time meeting the diverse needs, interests, and abilities of the students in their classrooms. Careful planning and

consideration are required to ensure that a balanced literacy program is in place. (Schwartz & Pollishuke, 2012, p. 177)

Jill has welcomed parents into the school and made them feel they are partners in their children's learning. Jill provides babysitters for parents with young children on literacy and math nights and for other school evening events. Teachers have begun to experiment with student-led conferencing so that for parents whose language is other than English, the students can not only translate but also explain what is important about their learning.

Jill is purposefully visible in halls and classrooms and the staff have slowly began more coherent enforcement of effective classroom behaviors. After Jill's first year as principal, suspensions declined as did incidents reported to the office. In the second year, academic results increased in reading and the staff and parents began talking about Pleasant Valley as a turn-around school. The halls and classrooms are now covered with student work, pictures of school teams and clubs, and messages such as "Success lives here at Pleasant Valley" and "Students are working here to succeed." The school is finally living up to its name. Increasingly, staff members are now more individually and collectively committed to the school improvement process after they saw the results of improvement in their classes and across their school. For the upcoming review, almost all of the school staff want to be involved.

Organizing for the Review

At the initial staff meeting, the staff brainstorm the various tasks that need to be done, and establish a series of subcommittees. Ownership for the review is building. The members of the school improvement team chair the subcommittees established to ensure an excellent review. Collectively, the staff discuss the key messages they want the external review team to understand about Pleasant Valley, and share these at parent council meetings and in the school newsletters and on the website:

- Acquisition and mastery of literacy and numeracy skills are the most important goals and they will be the focus of the school.
- Teachers have high expectations for their students' achievement and are committed to using student data formatively to inform their practices to boost achievement.
- The school is committed to targeted interventions for students with special needs and for students who are ELL.

To help further prepare, Jill brings a series of boxes to the staff room. Each is labeled with a goal from the school improvement plan and she invites staff over the next few weeks to bring in evidence that supports the realization of one of the school's SMART goals. In doing so, Jill and her staff discuss what effective learning looks like and sounds like. She says evidence could be a piece of student work, a photo, an assignment they created, an anchor chart, or minutes from one of the professional learning communities (PLCs). Jill is clear: it is their choice. The boxes will form the basis of the evidence they, as staff, want to share with the external review team. The subcommittees leave with the intent to establish mini–work plans for the tasks that need to be completed:

- Operations team. In charge of operational issues, this group decides that the library will close for the day of the review so that the external team members can have quiet, secure space. This will also give them needed room for the boxes of evidence being gathered. The operations group then begins working on the timetable for the day. They figure four teams for the eight external review members are needed to see all of the instructional spaces. The school day at Pleasant Valley runs from 9 to 3:15. They calculate that given the timetable there would need to be twenty-four classroom visits in total to ensure that physical education, health, music, and art will all be included. The decision had already been made that the morning coffee meet-and-greet and lunch for the external team will be provided centrally for the external team, so that isn't a cost or worry to the operations team. They consider posting signs showing the way to the review team's meeting room, library, and other key areas of the school, and include a map and timetable in the packages.

- Presentation team. This group decides they will create a video presentation and have a variety of staff talk about a specific aspect of school life. It will run for approximately fifteen minutes. They want to include student voice, so suggest that the Grade 6 class representatives do a brief presentation and that the school improvement committee ends with concluding remarks. The group will also develop some messages to share with the parent committee and to send home so that parents are kept in the loop. They will display a welcoming message on the day of the review on their billboard in front of the school.

- Data team. This group will track and record all of the evidence teachers place in the respective boxes and then organize it for the review team's evidence summary. They agree that teachers do not have to include their names and should also make sure there are no students' names on the materials. They want to include the results of a recent parent survey to demonstrate increased engagement and support. As a school, the Pleasant Valley grade teams' focus has been on guided reading, daily purposeful nonfiction writing, and problem solving with their classes using coconstructed materials. After Jill's four years, most faculty are now comfortable with moderated marking. The evidence summary will include results of pre- and posttests to demonstrate achievement as a result of staff adopting common approaches.

Jill poses questions to the staff to clarify their thinking: How are we going to present what we have accomplished together to the external review team? What evidence will we use to show what we are proud about? What areas do we want the review team to give us feedback on and suggest how we can continue getting better? She reiterates, everyone here has contributed and owns the results.

Areas for Focus and Feedback

Following the initial brainstorming, using the guiding questions from the reference group, the work of the subcommittees, and the data collected on student achievement, Pleasant Valley is ready to move forward. Collectively at a faculty meeting, they confirm Pleasant Valley's two areas of focus: a primary focus on emphasizing the balanced and comprehensive literacy program to support high levels of student achievement, and the other focus on using high-yield strategies to raise literacy achievement of all learners. Improving reading and writing and oral language skills is seen as foundational to all other learning. The faculty are more divided on areas for feedback. They are still working through their collective efforts in establishing effective classroom routines and strategies to support all students in a safe, inclusive, and positive learning environment. The challenge is what should come next.

Pleasant Valley has a large percentage of students receiving special education programs and services because, in addition to their own fully included students, they have some central self-contained classrooms where students are bused from other communities within the district. The school has a percentage of the ELL who are still struggling and underachieving, despite staff's high expectations and supports. Do they, as a staff, need to collectively work on establishing more effective formative assessment practices or should they emphasize timely and tiered interventions and build their expertise to support more inclusive classrooms? After much discussion, they select increasing their expertise to collectively respond to supporting inclusive classrooms using timely and tiered interventions, especially for students with special needs and ELL. They rationalize if they can better target interventions earlier, they will impact achievement.

Supporting Data

Now that the focus areas are established, each of the subcommittees go through the collected evidence—what would they keep and show? The process of developing a portfolio box is instructive. The data team examines each piece of evidence. They discuss:

- What does this piece of evidence say?
- How can it support one of the SMART goals?
- Is it valid and reliable?
- Will it add to the data tapestry of the school we are creating?
- Is it duplicating another piece of evidence?
- How much evidence is enough?

For their balanced literacy focus, Pleasant Valley has data from a variety of assessments, including the following: reading records for fluency, accuracy, and comprehension; data from the guided reading and writing sessions; data from commercially purchased assessments designed to determine and then level the student's individual reading and writing levels; books used for interactive read-alouds in the literacy room (Pinnell & Fountas, 2011); moderated

Reader Reflections

In your school, what are your areas of focus?

What data do you gather?

What data are you not gathering that you would like to?

Do the data help paint a data tapestry of achievement in your school? How would you describe the tapestry?

What types of evidence would you select to support areas for focus and feedback? Why?

What do data or evidence tell you about your progress to date in realizing your targets and goals?

What data conversations do you need to have?

marked samples of student work; large scale assessment data; and the report card data. For collective efforts in establishing effective classroom strategies that support all students in a safe, inclusive, and positive learning environment, Pleasant Valley—like other Lone Birch schools—tracks the following: demographic trend data, suspension data, incidents to the office, absenteeism, parent and student surveys, evidence from the in-school teams, partnerships to outside agencies and organizations, agendas and minutes of their learning teams, participation on school teams, as well as a host of other evidence (see Figure 4.2).

As the evidence is being selected, the other parts of preparation for the review team are also underway. The presentation team completes the video and, in the process, includes students and parents talking about aspects of school life. They also take pictures of the posted learning goals and success criteria. Building positive student leadership has helped build and maintain positive and safe learning environments, so the Grade 6 class representatives will do their own short presentation about student leadership and leadership opportunities offered through school clubs and teams. Pleasant Valley had previously decided to become an ecologically friendly school and the students want to talk about environmental awareness as part of their pride in the school, so the Grade 6 representatives will specifically address the ecology club in their presentation. The school improvement committee will end with concluding remarks. Now they are ready to present their plans to Dante, their school's supervisor.

Logistics

Two weeks before the review team is scheduled, Dante visits the school. Meeting with Jill and her school improvement team, they share their process

Figure 4.2 Evidence Summary for Pleasant Valley

From an analysis of the performance of students on the formalized assessments, report card data, running records, district assessments, parent surveys, attendance, and in-school meetings the following are noted:

Area of Focus and Feedback	Rationale for the Selection Area of Focus	Evidence in the School Improvement Plan	Evidence of Student Learning in Classrooms	Evidence in Public Spaces of the School (halls, offices, library, and other public spaces) and Messaging to Parents and Community	Additional Comments and Information
Focus Area 1: High-yield strategies are used intentionally and effectively to raise literacy achievement of all learners.	5% increase in reading, 3% in writing, and 6% in math on the formal assessments at Grades 3 and 6 Students in all grades making gains in reading fluency, accuracy, comprehension, and writing for meaning and purpose Improved results on questions asking students for their opinions or to justify their response through supporting materials from the text Responses on multiple-choice questions lower than short and long answers and perceptual data	Learning team focus on ELL and another on gender, exploring research on multiliteracies Provision for practice and consolidation at lunch and after school through homework clubs Reference to posters emphasizing academic	Dual-language texts reflective of the various linguistic/cultural groups, and graphic novels and current magazines available in the school libraries Separate boys' reading clubs and girls' reading clubs with posters Posted student writing samples with learning goals and success criteria attached	Students consulted on library texts;one of the highest circulation rates in LBSD; district messages included the hall signage and written in multiple languages for parents Pictures of students winning awards and other celebrations of student success	Support of the district ELL coach Looking at visiting other schools

(Continued)

Figure 4.2 (Continued)

Area of Focus and Feedback	Rationale for the Selection Area of Focus	Evidence in the School Improvement Plan	Evidence of Student Learning in Classrooms	Evidence in Public Spaces of the School (halls, offices, library, and other public spaces) and Messaging to the Parents and Community	Additional Comments and Information
	revealing anxiety of test-taking skills	vocabulary and subject-specific nomenclature	Consistent use of cocreated anchor charts and exemplars	Invitations to parent literacy nights	
	Increasing proportion of ELL students and the two dominant maternal languages other than English now Spanish and Mandarin		Posters emphasizing making connections using authentic examples that are culturally relevant	Dual-language texts in library/resource center	
	Gains for ELL in assessments on comprehension and writing process		Learning goals and success criteria in student-friendly language	Access to an English as a second language (ESL) teacher to build skills	
	Gaps remaining for gender, with concern about underachieving males complicated by issues of multiliteracy		Posters emphasizing academic vocabulary and subject-specific nomenclature	School requests for services from community workers	
				Partnerships with social service agencies	

Focus Area 2: The school has a balanced and comprehensive literacy program.	Gaps in reading comprehension on required assessments Gains in reading especially for at-risk readers with the focus on guided reading Analysis of running records showing a need for expansion of vocabulary and comprehension and gains made on fluency More comfort with oral response compared to written response in terms of reading for connections (text to text, text to self, text to world) Highest gains in persuasive writing More at-risk boys as readers and writers especially in areas of including enough relevant details to justify answers	Listed as a targeted strategy to support the SMART goal on literacy; Using specific literacy assessments to measure accuracy, fluency, and comprehension Uninterrupted literacy blocks Increase in student results measured on required reading and writing assessments Working on increasing student voice Dedicated professional learning teams exploring deep comprehension and oracy and multiliteracy strategies for ELL	Using balanced literacy—read-alouds, guided, shared, and independent; examples of moderated marking—samples of student work	Cocreated anchor charts, professional readings in library, pictures of teachers and student council reps reading their favorite books Wide variety of reading materials in the library	Lunch-and-learn sessions; using the system literacy coach

(Continued)

Figure 4.2 (Continued)

Area of Focus and Feedback	Rationale for the Selection Area of Focus	Evidence in the School Improvement Plan	Evidence of Student Learning in Classrooms	Evidence in Public Spaces of the School (halls, offices, library, and other public spaces) and Messaging to the Parents and Community	Additional Comments and Information
Focus Area for Feedback 1: Effective strategies that support all students in a safe, inclusive, and positive learning environment are established.	Initially had above the district average in suspensions and incidents to the office, had graffiti and more parental calls to the LBSD, and declining enrollment 10% decrease in suspension data and 10% increase in perfect attendance 20% increase in volunteers to act as peer mediators 5% decrease in incidents to office but still higher than the family of schools Increase in students participating in co-instructional activities,	Present statistics—tracking absenteeism suspensions, incidents to office, and demographic data—showing declines over the last three years; working on restorative justice; training peer mediators for recess; moving to balanced day since most off-behaviors occur	Cogenerated posted norms of positive classroom behaviors Ecological club drawn from every grade Positive classroom routines supported by monthly character assemblies Students advocating for what they require as learners Students working effectively together in diverse groupings	Positive messaging in the hall Posted exemplars—poems and short stories about bullying and other social justice themes Plaques celebrating student citizenship, citizenship award assemblies Messages to parents about bullying in the newsletter, available online through the school's website	Partnership with community police Partnerships with other community agencies Working to develop coaches

	especially sports teams and chess 10% increase in parental attendance at school-based activities	during the long lunch hour Parental and student survey results	Dual-language texts in library/resource center Information for parents posed in several languages (Spanish, Mandarin) in the halls and small section of the library devoted to resources for parents Reading nights with students Books in bags that are culturally responsive	Created a pilot for summer school units and summer reading and hoping to pilot a
Focus Area for Feedback 2: Timely and tiered interventions are provided.	Wide range of academics Housing some of the district self-contained special education classes 20% increase in the number of kindergarten students with high needs, according to data from the early intervention measures 10% increase in need for accommodations, as noted in IEPs	Establishing in-school team Looking to early identification Using a data wall to track underachieving students	Focus on homogeneous group for interventions and extensions as well as heterogeneous groupings Current student learning profiles	Created cross-discipline and cross-grade groupings for tutoring—notices and information up Information posted about pathways

(Continued)

Figure 4.2 (Continued)

Area of Focus and Feedback	Rationale for the Selection Area of Focus	Evidence in the School Improvement Plan	Evidence of Student Learning in Classrooms	Evidence in Public Spaces of the School (halls, offices, library, and other public spaces) and Messaging to the Parents and Community	Additional Comments and Information
	More students being brought to in-team meetings	IEPs reviewed on an ongoing basis			literacy summer camp
	Increase in the number of at-risk boys who are also ELL struggling with reading and writing process and skills	School team meetings scheduled to discuss at-risk learners			
	15% increase in requests by teachers and parents for assistive technology	Using marker students to track impact of interventions			
	8% increase in incidents of aggression in the special education classrooms				
	10% success with the early intervention programs shown in the decrease in off-task and self-regulating behaviors				

planning as a school, their suggested plans, and their selected evidence with Dante. He asks questions to support guided conversations and encourage thinking and reflection.[1] He will share the data at the senior team meeting.

Pleasant Valley's instructional day runs from 9:00 a.m. to 3:15 p.m. The operational team has calculated they require four teams or a total of eight external review team participants to visit all classes during their onsite visit, including some classes where the morning teachers teach a specialty subject. The observations will begin at approximately 9:05, after the presentation, and give the external team a chance to prepare. The first block will include four class visitations, then a thirty-minute break to debrief, and then three more classes and the break at lunch, and then a final three classes so that each team visits ten classes in total.

Dante likes what they have done and gives only a few minor suggestions about the selection of data and the scheduling. He wants to build in time for the review team to visit the library/resource center, and also the school's literacy and numeracy workroom. Both are integral parts of the school and the library/resource room is the hub for cross-grade and subject learning; it contains a growing professional library for staff because Jill wants students to see teachers reading too—it is an important message. Pleasant Valley is now good to go.

Meadows Middle School

Meadows Middle School, with 300 students in Grades 7–8, is not demonstrating improvement. In fact, its student achievement results are stuck, or in the case of mathematics, in decline. Its community and student base are similar to Pleasant Valley but located in a different area and family of schools of Lone Birch. Many students come from a lower socioeconomic background and the student population and their parents are transient; however, there is a more stable and affluent school community within the school's accommodation boundaries. The areas once housed a large factory, which was the chief employer. It closed and so did the jobs. People moved in search of viable employment opportunities. Approximately a third of the school's students speak a maternal language other than English at home—Spanish, Farsi, Urdu. Students are often late and appear bored, or talk back during class. Most homework assigned is never completed. Staff are in mourning for the "school that was."

When Mel came, the school had one of the highest suspension rates in Lone Birch. Mel, an experienced principal, had only been at Meadows Middle School for one year and requested the review as a potential lever for change. As Mel remarks to Dante, "Maybe they will listen to someone else's advice—they are not listening to me." Mel, like Jill, believes that all of the students at Meadows Middle have potential and can learn—the challenge is convincing staff. He wants to steer Meadows Middle in a more positive direction but needs the acknowledgment and support of staff.

Most of the faculty have been at Meadows Middle School for a long time. They teach with mainly traditional approaches: whole-class format, semi-lecture

---

[1]The questions can be found in the previous chapter.

style with students sitting in rows. Meetings are organized around subject departments. Staff at Meadows Middle are not meeting in learning teams. Under Mel's leadership, this is beginning to change. He believes that improving the quality of teaching will improve the quality of learning.

Staff maintain that they have high standards and their students' results are disappointing. It is an issue of student learning and not their teaching. Some staff feel that if parents were more involved and homework completed, then student marks would increase. Mel has found staff resistant to change. Only three staff volunteered to help draft the school improvement plan, which was presented at a staff meeting. Most teachers didn't see how its directions should influence their teaching. As one commented, "I teach science; literacy is the English department's job." For parent nights, the turnout is very low. Some teachers say it is because "they don't care about education." There is talk of offering a homework club for afterschool support using high school student volunteers, but nothing has yet materialized.

Organizing for the Review

Mel knows he will not get a lot of volunteers to help plan the collaborative school review so he personally asks five staff with whom he has developed a positive relationship. His school improvement team includes some teachers who are changing their instruction and assessment practices as well as others who see no need to change, but like Mel are willing to work on the planning for the collaborative school review. Unlike Pleasant Valley, where there are enough interested staff to form subcommittees, Mel and his team of five are responsible for everything.

Areas for Focus and Feedback

Mel uses the questions from the reference committee that Dante and Clay shared to focus the work of the group preparing the evidence summary. When the small group begins to look at their areas of strength to share with the external review team, they select the staff's high expectations for student achievement because they know they can get staff buy-in. The second area for focus they choose is ongoing communication to and engagement with parents. One of the younger staff members has even developed a new website. Staff feel they are really trying to communicate with parents, even if they don't get the results they expect. The district is working on formative assessment or assessment for learning, and while a few teachers are on board, it is not yet in place at Meadows Middle, so it is thus the first area they want feedback on. Linked to it is the challenge using data effectively to continuously monitor learning. Teachers mainly use their own individual classroom data to make decisions about student marks. Most assignments and tasks are commercially prepared blackline masters or worksheets. Only in a few classes are learning goals and success criteria posted. Staff collectively do not engage in data conversations or moderated practice.

The students at Meadows Middle are more diverse with different languages (Spanish, Farsi, and Urdu) and cultures. Staff aren't clear on how to accommodate for these differing needs. Some staff say the parents need to monitor homework. Lone Birch is also working on differentiation. Some offer choice in terms of product or topic selected for an assignment. Some talk about providing assistive technology or more time, but most staff are not clear how those strategies align to their current classroom practice and to the report card data. Differentiation of instruction and assessment become the next area for feedback. The Meadows Middle improvement team feels there will not be staff resistance to the two areas of focus and a manageable amount to the two for feedback.

Supporting Data

The need to gather evidence to support the areas for focus and for feedback results in lots of discussion. The issues are brought to a previously scheduled staff meeting. Staff divide into four groups, each with a specific potential area of focus and each group is asked to list the evidence that the review team should be given, if that area of focus is selected. Each staff member is given a copy of the school improvement plan and asked to highlight those parts that refer to their area for focus or feedback using different colored markers. The team given high expectations selects the pictures of students on the honor roll, students who have been successful in college or university, the ambitious targets in the school improvement plan, and the messages supporting student learning in the newsletter to parents. Some say they can share assignments and examples of their best students' work. For communication, staff say they have flyers advertising the opening barbecue, parents' night, and curriculum night; they also have copies of previous newsletters, minutes of the parent council, and the new website. They talk about the school's homework code, and key messages about working hard in class and completing homework that they emphasize in students' school agendas. The faculty are proud of the events they have organized to share information with parents. This leads to the team focused on communication also raising this issue, and why so few parents actually attend parents' night, curriculum night, and the parent council. Only the opening meet-and-greet barbecue was attended by the majority of parents. Are they not interested, or working multiple jobs, or do they not understand what teachers are trying to share? This last area is contentious. Some staff think parents don't care about the school and others think that the events are not responsive to parents' needs and do not provide translation for parents struggling with English. The highlighted school improvement plans are gathered as another way to find out what staff think are important.

Figure 4.3 shows the evidence summary for Meadows Middle School. The staff have now given their input, but the real work of gathering evidence, collating it, and presenting it is for Mel and his team of five. Ownership for learning is not yet shared.

For assessment for learning and using student data effectively to inform classroom practice, the suggestions from those teams is to share minutes from the professional learning. Mel has a few staff members willing to work as part of a learning team. Some staff use rubrics and success criteria but not all, so the suggestion is that for the staff using rubrics, the evidence package include pictures of the anchor charts, posted rubrics, or success criteria on

Figure 4.3   Evidence Summary for Meadows Middle School

Area of Focus and Feedback	Rationale for the Selection Area of Focus	Evidence in the School Improvement Plan	Evidence of Student Learning in Classrooms	Evidence in Public Spaces of the School (halls, offices, library, and other public spaces) and Messaging to the Parents and Community	Additional Comments and Information
Focus Area 1: The staff promote a culture of high expectations relaying that all students can learn, progress, and succeed.	History of past excellence—many staff were experienced Fifteen teachers with graduate degrees 8% increase of students participating in national math challenges Increase in student participation in band, art club, robotics club, and chess club 15% increase in results of the advanced math class Students graduating from the advanced math class demonstrating higher results on the formal math assessment in Grade 9; however Grades 7 and 9 math results declining, as reflected on report cards 10% increase in former students enrolled in university/college returning to offer mentoring to Grade 8 students	High expectations mentioned seven times in the school's SIP Offering advanced math classes as an extension opportunity Data gathered about student progress Math and science teachers working with their high school counterparts	Posted lists of students with As in the assignments, tests, and final grades in each class Teacher-bought posters with positive messaging about success	Posted lists of students with perfect attendance Posters about college/university opportunities in the halls Posters about successful global leaders Pictures of previous graduates, trophies, and plaques highly visible in the front hall—reflecting a school with traditions	

Focus Area 2: Parental engagement is encouraged and ongoing effective parent communication is evident.	Revised website and posted the school newsletter Four teachers with online blogs Information sent home in Spanish, Farsi, and Urdu Highest parent attendance over any meeting held in the last three years at parent night addressing transitions to high school 5% increase in parent attendance at school-based events 25% increase in hits on the school and class websites	One of the school's SMART goals Parental survey Hosted three curriculum nights as well as meetings with parents over report cards	References to the individual class and school's website in classrooms Samples of the school newsletter available	Section in front hall devoted to parents and the community Some limited parental resources in the library Former students now in college visiting to speak to the Grade 8 students	
Focus Area for Feedback 1: Formative assessment (assessment for learning) is used to inform teaching and learning.	Percentage of at-risk learners in Grades 6 to 8 remaining unchanged, as measured by report card data One of the PLCs exploring formative assessment	Listed as a strategy to support SMART goal in literacy One of the learning teams considering moderated marking Joint tests and exams created across departments Using teacher–student conferencing	Student work posted Using report card data on student placement Rubrics posted in classrooms Comments on report cards personalized to reflect the progress of individual students	Posted rubrics in the displays of science and math departments IEPs current and reflecting student's individual learning needs	Accessed the district's coaches

(Continued)

Figure 4.3 (Continued)

Area of Focus and Feedback	Rationale for the Selection Area of Focus	Evidence in the School Improvement Plan	Evidence of Student Learning in Classrooms	Evidence in Public Spaces of the School (halls, offices, library, and other public spaces) and Messaging to the Parents and Community	Additional Comments and Information
		Articles from the district on assessment for learning in staff handbook	Student portfolios for students at-risk being developed		
Focus Area for Feedback 2: Assessment and evaluation is differentiated to accommodate differing learning needs, styles, and abilities.	District focus 10% increase in the reported use of appropriate manipulatives and technology by students, as reported by teachers Students using technology to create their final project On IEPs, 10% of students with additional time for test taking and results for students with special needs showing some increase for problem solving	Strategy to support SMART goal in mathematics	Choice on products on assignments Students using technology to create their final product and completed projects posted in the computer lab Students working in flexible groups Posters on multiple intelligences		Accessed the district's coaches

the few classroom walls. At the staff meeting, the four groups make it clear—they will leave the gathering of the specific evidence to Mel and the improvement team planning for the collaborative school review.

Logistics

At this same staff meeting, several staff raise the issue that they are going to be uncomfortable having external people in their classrooms. Mel says he will ask Dante to speak with them. He reminds everyone that the reviews are not about individual staff members, or about appraisals and evaluation, but rather a way for the school to have feedback on where they are collectively on the improvement continuum. He texts Dante, who responds that he can return to the school at the end of classes on Thursday of that week, and respond to questions.

Because participation is limited, they decide that the improvement team will do the presentation and the timetabling for the day. Unlike Pleasant Valley, planning for the review is going to be in the domain of a few. Again, as he had at Pleasant Valley, Dante meets with Mel and his team of five for the discussion about preparing for the collaborative school review.

Meadows Middle School is smaller than the other two pilot schools. Their instructional day runs from 8:30 a.m. to 3:00 p.m. There will be two teams of three people, with twenty classes visited in total. The observations will begin at 9:05, after the presentation and, like Pleasant Valley, to give the external team a chance to prepare. The first block will include three class visitations, then a thirty-minute break to debrief, and then four classes and the break at lunch, and then a final three classes so that each team visits ten classes total.

Dante and Mel meet with the interested staff. Dante reiterates Mel's messages and reminds them that the union/federation had been part of the initial planning process. He assures them no teacher will be named, the external review team members will not write during their classroom observations, and will try and be as minimally disruptive as possible. When members of the external review team enter the teachers' classrooms, the teachers can choose to introduce the team or simply ignore them. It will be the teachers' choice. All staff will be invited to a breakfast to meet the external review team the day of the review, and attendance for the verbal debriefing at the end of the day is voluntary. All staff will be involved in the unpacking of the written report and part of the decision making on how the review team's findings can be effectively implemented. That process is not yet established at Meadows Middle School. Mel is determined that the review process will be a lever for needed change; however, he is cognizant of the tension that exists among staff.

Harper High School

If Pleasant Valley staff are anticipatory and Meadows staff reluctant, Harper High School staff can hardly wait. The school is located in the most affluent area of the district and has a reputation for high academics and being a "good school." While staff are pleased that their student results are positive, they do not rest on their laurels. From "good to great" is their slogan. Based on student scores, they could be complacent. On the assessments, 89 percent of students are at or above standard. For credit completion, 87 percent of students in Grade 9 and 85 percent of students in Grade 10 are not at academic risk, having successfully completed eight of their required eight credits. Post-secondary data shows 88 percent of students have applied to post-secondary and most are successful in attending the institution of their first choice. Graduates from universities regularly come back to talk about their university experiences and how Harper High prepared them for success.

Organizing for the Review

Under Annie's leadership, the teachers have been working collaboratively in learning teams for over five years. Annie has been at the school for seven years working closely with Juan, the school's supervisor. She came to education late, working as a management consultant in a large corporation. Annie brought those skills into her present role. She sees herself as a creative and supportive leader. She is a visible leader and frequently observed in classrooms. Annie developed and sustains shared leadership. Initially she built trust, and then used her observational data and the achievement data to ask challenging and reflective questions so that staff was not complacent: Which students were not succeeding at Harper High? How did they know? Why was it happening? What then changed in terms of teaching and learning? The guiding questions developed by the reference team help, but Annie has been using similar questions all along, influenced by Levin's (2012) work on reforming high schools to improve achievement.

From her management perspective, data matter. Annie used the analysis from the student data to create a data tapestry to have data dialogues and to raise potentially controversial discussions for staff's consideration, such as whether Grade 9 math should be taught in a block/semester timetable or throughout the year, and what made technology assistive and necessary for some students. In terms of interventions, what impacted achievement? Was the same good for all students or which students required a targeted approach? She reads widely, and shares research in terms of effective instructional practices. Annie knows she has to model what she expects for staff. Juan says she has a "learning stance."

Annie, with the support of Juan, her supervisor, and the system coaches, has organized the staff into learning teams as well as their traditional subject-based departments. Once a month, Annie negotiates an hour late start to the instructional day for students and teachers to work collaboratively in learning teams. Parents are onboard because achievement remains high and more students want to come to the school than can be accommodated. Unlike Meadows Middle School, Harper High School is a school of choice. The school improvement plan was developed collaboratively over an entire year and staff shared ideas in designing the framework to guide change. Annie, like Lea, believes that successful plans "are short and organic." Knowing that not all students at Harper High will be successful, all students entering in Grade 9 are assessed in reading, writing, and mathematics and interventions put into place for those students requiring extra support. Staff volunteered and ran afterschool programs including homework help called "topping up." Peer tutors train and are available during the lunch period and after school in an initiative called "learn2learn." Tutoring is a credit and looks good on college applications, so there is no shortage of tutor volunteers. In-school team support meetings run every week to discuss students who have begun to struggle academically or socially. There are a wide variety of leadership opportunities for students, including a commitment to the Me to We–Free the Children outreach. Student data is regularly gathered and deconstructed to inform decision making. The in-school team meets regularly. Staff know that among the students who are underachieving, there are more females than males at Harper High, which is not the general pattern in the district.

Areas for Focus and Feedback

In their learning teams, Harper High staff have already selected their areas for focus and feedback. They are committed to building their skills and expertise collectively. Each teacher identified marker students who are struggling to follow and work with on interventions. The school is experimenting with clear learning goals and big ideas to frame students' learning. The departments modified these to meet subject-specific as well as common criteria. These and the rubrics and success criteria are beginning to be cocreated. Most classes have posted rubrics, learning goals, and anchor charts as well as other cuing systems.

The first area of focus to celebrate is that student results are up. Teachers feel this is because of the ongoing collaborative work they had been doing in their learning teams. They also choose to focus on their ongoing and deliberate use of valid and reliable student achievement data to inform teachers' practice. Staff in their learning groups have been talking about developing higher-order thinking and creating rich tasks, but are unsure of how regularly these strategies are being used. Teachers want feedback on the use of high-order thinking and critical thinking practices across the schools. Teachers believe that they champion student learning but are still not there, so they select equitable and inclusive practices as an area for feedback. The student population is becoming more diverse and teachers want to make sure they are respectful and responsive to students' needs. This is thus selected as the second area for feedback.

Supporting Data

Now the issue is what evidence will they gather to support the areas for focus and feedback. This is left to the school improvement team to manage with assistance from the subject departments, although staff is helpful with suggestions including the following:

- The assessments used in Grade 9 to identify potential at-risk students
- Data on the student success indicators
- The lists of interventions used to support students

- Departments engaged in moderated marking—meeting agendas and minutes
- Cogenerated learning goals, exemplars, success criteria, and other cuing systems
- The fact that classrooms regularly post student work
- The beginning use of descriptive feedback on the posted student work
- The use of student portfolios in some classes
- The regular use of student–teacher conferencing for feedback
- The electronic data walls used to track improvement
- Adding dual-language resources in the library and asking students to suggest resources the library should acquire

The organization and gathering of specific data is left to the department heads and curriculum chairs. They and the school improvement team meet with Juan, their school supervisor, for the prereview meeting. Juan has the feedback from Dante's meetings at Pleasant Valley and Meadows Middle. He is impressed with Harper High's synergy. In a school that draws from high socioeconomic strata and has always been academic, it is easy for staff to believe that high achievement results from their excellent teaching and not social capital. While some believe it is their high expectations for students that impact student achievement, others acknowledge the parents have equally high expectations for their children. Annie and her team make sure that, as she says, "The staff have ongoing reality checks." They work together to create the evidence summary chart (see Figure 4.4).

Logistics

The media classes have created a five-minute video the school will use, full of student voices talking about what they see as strengths and weaknesses at Harper High. The student council will act as guides on the day of the review because the school is large by Lone Birch standards. It has undergone several revisions and rooms are not numbered in a systematic way; finding specific rooms, even with a school map, could be time consuming and frustrating for the external review team and take time away from focused classroom observations.[2] Teams will be allocated a specific wing or floor so time isn't wasted going up and down floors. The departments have gathered their evidence of effective practices and there will be a few examples of student and teacher work placed on display in the room reserved for the external team; they could peruse this at their leisure during the day. Staff are proud of what they are accomplishing and proud of their students' accomplishments. To illustrate, the improvement team at Harper High prepares an electronic synopsis for the external review team, which they will send out in advance and there will also be a package waiting when they arrived for the onsite visit.

---

[2]We have been on reviews where the school is very large (2,500 plus students) and undergone additions and even with a map, too much time is wasted locating a specific class. In these types of schools, consider using student leaders as guides.

Figure 4.4 Evidence Summary for Harper High School

Area of Focus	Rationale for the Selection Area of Focus	Evidence in the School Improvement Plan	Evidence of Student Learning in Classrooms	Evidence in Public Spaces of the School (halls, offices, library, and other public spaces) and Messaging to the Parents and Community	Additional Comments & Information
Focus Area 1: Professional learning is collaborative, school-based, and drawn from the data; uses an inquiry approach; builds individual and collective capacity; and informs practice.	Established learning teams on literacy, problem solving and thinking, safe and secure schools, and equity—with teams using a collaborative inquiry approach	Learning team strategy in the SIP across departments	Cogenerated anchor charts and rubrics posted	Pictures of student teams	Providing agendas of learning teams
		In-school team meetings to work collaboratively, including special education, guidance, co-op, and the vice principals	Posted learning goals	Pictures of staff working together in the staff room	
	Cross-department learning teams targeting at-risk learners with 87% of students in Grade 9 and 85% in Grade 10 not academically at-risk, and 18% decrease in at-risk learners over three years	Two teachers working on a master's degree in collaborative learning using research based on the school	Regular student–teacher conferencing	Leadership opportunities for students posted	
			Working on consistent instructional practices classroom to classroom		
	10% decline in suspensions	Ongoing data used to identify at-risk learners in grades and subjects, with	Students working collaboratively on problem solving		
	Increase in the use of technology in student learning,				

(Continued)

Figure 4.4 (Continued)

Area of Focus	Rationale for the Selection Area of Focus	Evidence in the School Improvement Plan	Evidence of Student Learning in Classrooms	Evidence in Public Spaces of the School (halls, offices, library, and other public spaces) and Messaging to the Parents and Community	Additional Comments & Information
	resulting from strategies developed by a cross-department learning team exploring the International Baccalaureate (IB) program and 21st-century learning	weekly meetings to discuss and program for at-risk learners identified by staff			
	20% increase in students seeking help at the Topping-Up program organized across subject areas	Department chair meetings monthly to look at areas of common direction and planning			
	88% of students graduating applied to postsecondary institutions	Department heads coordinating Topping-Up program and peer-tutoring program called Learn2learn			
Focus Area 2: Data is aggregated and	Programming decisions made that were not evidence driven	Gathered, disaggregated, and analyzed data	Portfolios in use across several departments	Posted student work	Use of electronic data walls

114 ●

| disaggregated to inform decision making. | Student profiles used to track students at risk of not receiving a credit and 15% decrease in students in Grades 9 and 10 who are unsuccessful in terms of achieving credits

Emphasis on learning goals and success criteria resulting in an increase in students understanding the relationship between what they are learning, how they have acquired the learning, and how it connects to their schema

18% increase in the number of graduates being accepted to their first choice of university/college | Assessments from every Grade 9 to identifying at-risk students

Using marker students

Data on key indicators recorded and shared across staff | | | |
|---|---|---|---|---|---|
| Focus Area for Feedback 1:

The teaching and learning environment promotes equity and respect and | Increasing incidents of reported bullying

ELL students underperforming on the formal assessments

Perceptional data from equity audit revealing that students from visible minorities feel marginalized | Support for Me to We program and a sister school in Kenya

Results from student and parental surveys

Using a variety of interventions | Clubs and speakers supporting issues of equity and social justice

Dual-language books in the libraries

Some teachers experimenting with | Poster regarding peer tutors

Student input sought on suggestions for the library | Partnerships with the community

Speakers in from the community presenting to |

(Continued)

Figure 4.4 (Continued)

Area of Focus	Rationale for the Selection Area of Focus	Evidence in the School Improvement Plan	Evidence of Student Learning in Classrooms	Evidence in Public Spaces of the School (halls, offices, library, and other public spaces) and Messaging to the Parents and Community	Additional Comments & Information
uses culturally appropriate resources, practices, and processes.	Attitudinal surveys reporting that 33% students don't feel the school promotes diversity and equity Equity audit revealing that most oral and written examples for students do not reflect their lived experiences 12% increase in students of color being bullied, as reported to the office and student peer leaders 60% of staff reporting at the awareness and beginning stages in terms of implementing differentiation	Tracking achievement gaps Promoting diversity through appointing school leaders and staff hires Equity resource staff from Lone Birch speaking at staff meetings	culturally responsive pedagogy Students reporting on attitudinal survey that they see themselves more reflected in the examples used in the curriculum than in previous years	Gathering of student input for decisions on school priorities	students at lunch time

Focus Area for Feedback 2: Higher-order thinking skills are used to increase complexity in thinking.	Higher-order and critical thinking skills being used to increase complexity in learning	Learning team with higher-order thinking as a focus	Higher-order thinking skills being taught and integrated across subject areas	Chess, math, robotics, and gaming clubs	Some consideration of the IB program being explored
	25% increase in accountable talk and student engagement, as reported by staff collaborating on rich tasks in their learning group	Departments reviewing their exams to ensure higher-order questions are included	Posters on higher-order and critical thinking skills	Published list of student leadership activities	
	10% of students on assessments more able to identify and solve multistep problems and cross-curricular problems	Exploring the IB program	Teachers asking open-ended questions		
	13% increase from last year for students receiving As on their report cards	Attendance by two staff at workshop on how to make thinking visible	Students working with real-world data		
	8% increase over the last three years in students achieving at or above standard on the formal assessments		Extension activities available for students		
	Advanced math and science students ranked as top district performers on the university-sponsored national contests		Discussion of ethical issues involving social media		
			Student access to a variety of technologies to research, explore, and document learning		

The school reviews are scheduled in three week intervals to allow the key participants' time to reflect and regroup and for Clay to complete the individual reports. The staff at Harper High complete their evidence summary and send it electronically to Clay, as the system lead. Given that there are 800 students at Harper High, the plan is for an external review team of twelve, including Clay, ensuring the six subgroups visit all instructional spaces. Clay and Juan, the school's supervisor, are part of the team as well as four of Lone Birch's current high school principals, two elementary principals, one middle school principal with expertise in special education, and the system coordinator for literacy. Mel, the principal of the Meadows Middle, and Jill, the principal of Pleasant Valley, are also on the team. This way the schools who are still preparing for their review will get a chance to see the process unfold. It also is a way to build leadership capacity among the principals and strengthen their networks. A week prior to the actual visit, members of the team will receive a package including the school's improvement plan, a synopsis of the achievement data, and their evidence summary highlighting the areas of focus.

At Harper High, the school day runs from 8:45 a.m. to 3:00 p.m. to facilitate a complex bus schedule in the district. There will be six teams of twelve external reviews who will visit eleven classes on a four class, three class, and then four class schedule. Some of the teams will have a blank period to accommodate the master schedule but they will visit every instructional space, including the portables.

For the three schools and Lone Birch it is now all systems go.

Reader Reflections

For the three pilot schools, what would you have done differently?

Was there something that you would add or leave out? Why?

Consider using these three pilot schools as a way to begin conversations in your school or district.

IN SUMMARY

This chapter has focused on the planning at the school level. This is just as critical as the planning at the system level. In fact, a key demarcation of collaborative school reviews is the emphasis on collaborative planning with school staff. We believe that the real value in collaborative school reviews lies in the unleashing of staff to provide their ideas and suggestions. It is in the joint review of data and the discussion of the external review team's observations that valuable insights about possible changes in teaching practices surface. The planning for the school review needs to build the environment that engages and involves staff in the review process and the development of findings and opportunities for improvement. Developing the plan at a school level involves identifying all the activities that need to take place and working out how these will be done.

As you implement the Common Core State Standards, or work on increasing complexity and creating rich tasks to promote student thinking and student voice, consider having staff create the indicators or look-fors that can go into an evidence summary. The process allows for focused conversations on the use of data and the results of data analysis. It keeps the emphasis on collaboration with teaching and learning. The plan at the school level needs to detail each step that will be taken and the logistics. This includes preparation for the onsite visit, the onsite visit, and the debriefing. Thus each school needs a detailed work plan for each school that specifies how the school will prepare for their review, the data they will be using, logistics for the day of the review, and a follow-up plan. Select the school most like yours and adapt what the Lone Birch schools have done to meet your own unique needs.

For further information and additional resources, please visit the website associated with this book at www.collaborativeschoolreviews.com.

5 The Day of the Review

Linda Darling-Hammond (2010) argues that accountability, standards, and tests do not predicate improvement, but rather "improvements depend on greater teacher, school and system learning about more effective practice, combined with more equal and better targeted resource allocation" (p. 73).

Collaborative school reviews are about shared learning.

This chapter examines three components of conducting the collaborative school review: introduction and setting the stage, conducting the onsite review, and debriefing and sharing of findings and feedback (see Figure 5.1).

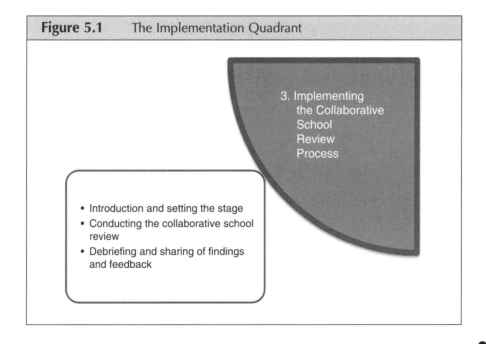

Figure 5.1   The Implementation Quadrant

3. Implementing the Collaborative School Review Process

- Introduction and setting the stage
- Conducting the collaborative school review
- Debriefing and sharing of findings and feedback

If attention has been paid to conceptualizing and designing the collaborative school review process as per Quadrant 1 and if the intentional planning envisioned in Quadrant 2 has occurred, then implementation in Quadrant 3, the implementation quadrant, is a natural progression; it fulfills the vision for strategically using collaborative school reviews within the district to bring about systemic and progressive improvements in student achievement. This does not mean that unforeseen issues will not occur—possible problems may arise, resulting in adjustments to the plan. What it does mean is that most of the pitfalls should have been considered and that there are both a plan and a backup plan. Additionally, the system and specifically the staff at the school level have developed an appreciation of what is to come and have been engaged in developing their school-based plan. In other words, the groundwork has been done and we are ready to move forward with interest, focused intent, and synergy. This should now be something that the district and its schools are doing jointly as a system and they should be proceeding with a shared vision, commitment, and understanding.

Effective implementation of the collaborative school review process requires that all stakeholders are properly introduced to the process and informed about what will happen, how it will happen, and when. All stakeholders should be aware of the expectations and how the finding and outcomes will be managed. During implementation, teams must continuously monitor and manage the work plan to ensure that any changes to the established plan are negotiated in a collaborative and inclusive manner so that there are no surprises. It is essential that continued engagement and support for the work to be done is sustained so that no one gets left behind. Effective implementation requires adherence to policy prerogatives, fidelity to process design, following protocols, and strict discipline around measuring progress and reporting outcomes. Remember, the school staff and the administration being reviewed will be understandably nervous. They want the external review team to see them in the best possible light. Although the messaging has been clear that this process is not about teaching, some teachers will be tense, others may be resistant or cynical, and not all will have bought into the process. Be realistic but positive. The more collaborative work done on the design and planning quadrants, the more stakeholders should be on board.

We discuss each of the components of Quadrant 3 through the lens of our case study. You will see the organic developments of the findings as you read through the Lone Birch onsite visits in each school. The findings are based on each series of observations, and deeper understanding of the school evolves as the observations are layered and the review team engages in conversation about what they hear and see. It is the gestalt arising from the combination of the observational data with the conversations that brings out the value of the collaborative school review. The challenges for the external review team are to convert that into clear, focused, and useful feedback at the end of the day of observation, as well as in the formal reports that are produced and submitted.

 Looking In

Harper High

After the months of planning and discussion, the date for the first review at Harper High has finally arrived.

Introduction and Setting the Stage

Clay and the selected external review team receive their package, review it individually, and then meet to examine the evidence summary and achievement data. Clay talks about the classroom observation materials the reference team has prepared, the types of questions to ask students, and areas to focus their observational lens. Clay reminds them of the following protocol:

- Arrive early.
- Smile and engage the school staff during the meet-and-greet. As Clay states, "We want the experience to be positive."
- Keep cell phones on vibrate when in classrooms and during presentations. They will be given designed time to respond to urgent messages.
- Keep the focus on the review and the school being visited and do not discuss other issues with the external review team members.
- Remember the issues of confidentiality.
- Be nonjudgmental and purposeful in their comments.
- Be specific and use examples from the observations to reference the evidence.
- Return the materials provided during the onsite visit so Clay can gather and shred anything confidential, and begin to prepare the written report.

These are part of the protocols established in the planning phase described in Chapter 2. Once these reminders are relayed, the team discusses some trends they observed arising from the data. Juan talks about the steady improvement at Harper High in the last six years since Annie has been appointed principal. All incoming Grade 9 students are now assessed when they enter and most are succeeding. As detailed in Chapter 4, on mandatory external assessments, 89 percent of students are at or above standard and 87 percent of students in Grade 9 and 85 percent of students in Grade 10 have completed eight of their eight required credits. In Grade 12, 88 percent of students applied to post-secondary schools and most were successful in attending the institution of their first choice. That left 13 percent of students in Grade 9 and 15 percent of students in Grade 10 who had not achieved their eight credits despite interventions such as credit rescue and recovery. Most of these students are male, face challenges in literacy comprehension, and tend to be reluctant readers and writers. Many are involved in co-op or experiential education and have selected courses dealing with broad-based technology, but their literacy skills are not high enough for the apprenticeship programs available in their area. Based on this data, the external review team debates how they might focus the observations to drill deeper into questions that the data raise. They plan to regroup early in the morning of the first onsite visit and have some additional discussion time prior to the first set of classroom visits. At that time, Clay will also take the external review team through any additional information provided by Harper High's improvement team and the district protocols for school reviews.

It's still dark at 7:30 a.m. when Annie arrives extra early to make sure that all is ready. A seminar room off the library is reserved for the day for the external review team. She, Juan, and the improvement team have gone over the schedules and the packages the school prepared. One of the teachers is absent, and as part of the design agreements, the supply teacher would not form part of the observations so those classes will be missed. Clay has multiple copies of the forms to be used in the classroom observations, clipboards, and extra pens. Packages have been prepared for each of the members containing the following:

- Timetable for the school
- Map of the school with washrooms and the room reserved for the external review team clearly marked
- A badge to wear as a visitor for security purposes
- The schedule for classroom observations for each of the six groups with a change noted because of a teacher absence
- The latest school newsletter
- The school improvement plan
- The results of the self-assessment survey
- The evidence summary
- The range of clubs, sports teams, and other leadership opportunities for students
- A list of events hosted by the school this semester
- The results of the latest student attitude survey
- Agendas from the last two parent committee meetings
- Topics covered in the ongoing professional learning scheduled for the school year

The coffee and tea are on, and Annie and her committee set out the healthy snacks. The video—the media students had prepared—is loaded into the SMART Board, and one of the committee members checks that it is working properly. All is ready.

Conducting the School Review

By 8:00 a.m. all members of the external team arrive for Clay's initial briefing. The packages and forms have been distributed to the external review team members. Clay and Juan divide the members into teams of two. Juan, as the school's supervisor, talks about the context and climate of Harper High. He and Clay quickly review the materials from the last meeting.

When the external review team initially met, they looked for patterns and trends from the student achievement data, which indicated that some males were not performing in reading and writing at the same levels as the female students. This was compounded for those male students for whom English was not their maternal language, so Clay also asks them to pay attention to underachieving students, especially boys in terms of reading materials, writing tasks, their work habits, and questions posed to them. Students at Harper High for the most part come from affluent homes and have parents with high expectations for college, so another area Clay wants them to pay attention to during the classroom observations is the degree of complexity and the use of higher-order thinking questions and tasks: Are these being used intentionally to support high achievement? If the students in Harper High are moving to higher levels of academic achievement, then the intentional and coherent use of rich and complex tasks is a necessity. Clay again reinforces the protocols for the classroom observations. He asks the external review team to pay attention to the areas of focus for Harper High including looking for evidence of the use of effective instructional strategies and cocreated anchor charts, exemplars, and other cuing systems across classrooms that are mentioned in their evidence summary. He reminds them to look for evidence in terms of how the ongoing work of the professional learning teams might manifest: What would be evidence that the review team might see not only in one classroom but across classrooms and subject areas? There are high expectations for students in this school and teachers recognize the need for higher-order thinking. In terms of complexity, Clay asks them to consider if the tasks students are working on are worth doing: Are the tasks rich? Are they open-ended allowing for multiple answers and encouraging student thinking? Are teachers focused on students completing the work or really understanding the task?

It is 8:15 and now time to join the staff in the library for the meet-and-greet and the briefing presentation. In the library, most of the Harper High staff are there and Juan introduces the members of the external review team, reviews the purpose of the day, and stresses that Lone Birch is a learning system and that collaborative school reviews form part of that learning process. By 8:30 staff required in classrooms have left and the presentation begins.

The student video shows members of the student council asking a variety of students from Grades 9–12 what they as students see as strengths of Harper High and then shows a clip illustrating that strength. The students also talk about challenges such as getting participation for some events and involving students meaningfully in volunteer activities the community partnerships established. Then a member of the school's improvement team highlights from the evidence summary those areas where the staff see areas of strength and areas they want feedback on. Annie reviews the additional information the external team has been provided with that morning and the plans for the day; she tells groups that each will have a member of the student council to be their guide because the observations are spread across all three floors of the school. By the time the presentation ends, the external review team has a few minutes in the seminar room to organize for their visits.

The lessons are underway as the review team goes to their first classes shortly after 9:00. In a few classrooms, the teacher directs the lessons while the external review members listen and walk the room observing the classroom environment, resources, and materials posted on chart paper and on the walls. They look at students' notebooks as the teacher is talking. In one class, students take notes from their textbook and in others they work in small groups on common tasks. In those classes where students work independently or interdependently, the members of the external review team use the list of possible questions vetted by the reference group to ask students to begin to drill down in terms of student learning. As mentioned in Chapter 4 on school-based planning, in a large school, having student council members as guides makes the transition from one class to another much easier and time isn't wasted finding the right classroom.

After their first four classroom observations, the team reassembles in the seminar room. Clay leads the debriefing session during the thirty minutes provided. He asks each pair to share a synopsis of their observations and the evidence the team saw in terms of the areas of focus. He uses a secure memory key to record the information shared on his laptop. Once all of the groups have reported, Clay asks probing questions, such as the following:

- What were your initial general impressions of Harper High?
- What evidence did you see or hear that provides information about the areas for focus and feedback?
- What patterns or trends did you see across the four classes in terms of the areas for focus and feedback?
- What did the students say when you asked your questions?
- Did you ask probing questions to drill down? What did you ask? What were the responses?
- What should we be paying attention to in the next set of classroom observations?
- Were there any challenges with the classroom observations?

Clay also keeps notes in the template that he created to collect feedback (refer back to Figure 3.6 in Chapter 3). This will be used for the verbal debrief and the written report. Juan too keeps notes for his own records.

After the debriefing, the teams are ready for their next set of three observations. This time the library, gym, and technology classes are on the list.

The break will be at lunch and provide another chance for the external review team to share their observations and develop preliminary findings. Clay continues to take the notes and poses questions to prod and keep the team on track.

The team decides to take some dedicated time to eat and catch up on their smartphones, and then debrief. This time the external review team looked at what was similar to and what was different from their original morning observations. There is heated discussion: Were students engaged in the tasks or just attentive to the task and what was the difference? Were tasks rich or rote-based? Was there a difference between experiential classes (technology, visual arts, band, and gym) and more traditional less experiential classrooms? Did they see or hear open-ended complex questions or tasks aimed at the higher end of Bloom's taxonomy? Clay reminds them that you cannot have higher-order and critical thinking if standards, tasks, and questions are only grounded at the comprehension and knowledge level. Complex thinking requires complexity in the tasks and questions about what students are doing. These are flagged in the school's evidence summary.

Did they see posted learning goals and success criteria? What were their observations in the congregated classrooms for students with complex special needs? What did they observe for students with IEPs integrated into regular classrooms for most of the day? Was the use of assistive technology obvious? In Student Service, what was being provided for students who were involved in recovering an incomplete credit from a previous term or rescuing one that they had already fallen behind in? It is in asking the questions and engaging in these types of discussions that the external review team realizes that they are learning too.

The team notes that students were on task in classrooms and not wandering the halls during class time. The team agrees that in most classes, students were working in pairs or groups and not sitting in rows. In several classrooms, students were working using rubrics but these were mainly teacher-created and the format of the rubric appeared common across classrooms. During the improvement team's briefing and in the evidence summary, the external review team was informed that Harper High teachers are working on using descriptive feedback and this was evident in a few classrooms based on teacher feedback and a scan of students' notebooks. Few teachers took the time to be explicit so that students knew how to move to the next level, but most feedback in the notebooks and on student work was motivational (good work) or corrective (mistakes circled). When asked, students for the most part knew what they were learning, but were not as sure about why it was important to learn that particular skill or concept. Most classrooms posted anchor charts (mainly teacher-created or bought), some had current examples of student work, and on those posted examples of student work many had the learning goals and rubrics included; however many classes had bare walls. These were all areas that the evidence summary claimed that the staff had been working on together. Many teachers were using real-world or authentic examples in their lessons to illustrate points. The only real differentiation observed was in terms of a limited choice of tasks or the group of students to work with. Most of the tasks assigned or questions asked appeared to be at the knowledge and comprehension levels.

In several classes, technology—such as interactive whiteboards, YouTube clips, blogs, and tweets—was being used in innovative ways. Teachers had a desktop and some laptop computers. Some students had their own personal computers and many of these had individual education plans or IEPs. There were several computer labs and a bank of computers in the library and all were being used. The library, they learned, was going digital in a big way. E-books were being considered as part of a pilot and the library contained a growing collection of male-friendly graphic novels and magazines. Students had input into the selection of library resources through their student council.

The external review team shares that students appeared to be more engaged in the experiential classes such as music, visual and dramatic arts, broad-based technologies, gym, weight training, and dance than regular traditional academic ones, where they were attentive and on-task but not necessarily actively engaged in their learning. While the library contained a good selection of resources to appeal to many levels, genres, and interests, classroom resources were more traditional. In most classes, the team found students working from the same textbook on the same task.

Clay and Juan keep the conversations focused and nonjudgmental. For administrators trained "to fix," not being critical is difficult. This is one of the features that distinguish collaborative reviews from traditional reviews. The team uses the evidence summary, what was observed, and the notes Clay was recording to begin to sketch out findings. What they observed was consistent with the first set of classroom visits in the morning.

It is now time for the final three observations. The team members are feeling more confident about their observations, and the sharing during the final external team debrief clarifies the patterns and trends observed earlier. The major focus is: What is similar and what is different in these sets of observations?

Debriefing and Sharing Findings and Feedback

When all the members of the external review team return, the students who acted as guides are thanked. Clay uses a data projector provided by Harper High to outline the key points that will be made during the verbal feedback session at the end of the school day for the entire staff. Clay structures this component into three activities: meeting with review team to organize and deliver findings and feedback, debriefing with the school administrative team, and meeting with all staff.

For each of the areas of focus, the initial feedback is positive with one or two areas for staff to think about. Clay then asks each member of the review team to address the following:

- Give the school two pieces of advice that would impact student learning.
- Provide one idea they will be taking back to share with their colleagues.
- What could make the learning or their participation as a member of the external review team better?

The external review team observed areas the evidence summary had highlighted such as anchor charts, learning goals, use of effective instructional strategies, and students working interdependently. However, the consensus from the external review team is that despite the work on complexity noted in the evidence summary, most questions and tasks were at the low level of Bloom's taxonomy and they agree that teachers need to think about creating rich tasks that are open-ended and require student thinking to make the learning more complex. These are needed to develop and reinforce critical thinking skills. One team member reflects, "Thinking wasn't visible." She is reading *Visible Learning for Teachers* (Hattie, 2012) and she is using the concepts presented in the book with her staff. The consensus among the team is that the students are capable and are not really being challenged to reach their full potential.

The external review team saw some evidence of descriptive feedback and suggests this as an area for staff to drill deeper and become more coherent. They suggest a refocus on differentiation and a consideration of some gender-specific interventions for the at-risk boys indicated in the school's data and who appeared to be disengaged in some classrooms. They want the school to continue to use technology as an enabler to increase engagement and relevance, and continue to use authentic and real-world examples. Another member suggests a focus on 21st-century learning. All agree, during the entire day, that the vast majority of students were on-task and the relationships between students and staff appeared respectful.

The principals on the external review team say they will look at their own school differently, especially in terms of the coherent and intentional use of higher-order thinking and differentiation. The issue of making learning visible is meaningful. In their minds, they begin to scope out preparations for their own onsite visit. The issue of seeing coherent practice resonates with a few of the principals. The system coaches are discouraged because they thought they would see lots of examples of the areas Lone Birch had been working on. The school-based team members were taking home different things to share at their own schools that Harper High had done well—how the departments collectively approach rubrics, the posting of anchor charts, and the use of technology. Everyone learned something worthwhile. Their school improvement lenses have been enhanced.

In terms of improving or revising the external review team process, no one has an immediate suggestion for improvement, but say they will ponder and e-mail Juan and Clay later. They appreciated seeing teaching and learning at another school. They liked the initial briefing and debriefing sessions and the focused conversations that Clay crafted. They plan to use some of the questions for students in their own instructional walks. It was, all agreed, an excellent day.

Annie and her administration team are invited in to hear the preliminary findings prior to the verbal feedback for all staff. This is to respectfully acknowledge the role of administration in instructional leadership. The prebriefing for administration was part of the initial design process. Annie knows her staff and how the messages will be received, and Clay and

Juan value her input. The consensus is that Harper High is doing many things right. There is evidence of staff collaboration because they saw common strategies in use across grades and departments. However, the team feels that although the students are performing well as indicated on the student achievement data sets, they are capable of much more. Most students are performing at a B or Level 3, but given the sociodemographics and the current academic success, students are capable of more complexity and critical thinking. The external review team feels that the students could benefit from a schoolwide intentional focus on increased complexity and rigor in the tasks and questions at the higher levels of Bloom's taxonomy. "Good to great" is the reoccurring theme that the external review team delivers for Harper High. Another area for suggestion is for teachers in learning teams to collectively explore differentiation because it isn't obvious in the observations they saw beyond students being given choices of topic or product.

Some members of the external review team opt to stay for the verbal sharing with staff but some need to leave—they have meetings or a crisis demanding their attention. The Harper High staff were invited to attend; however, attendance is voluntary as per the design at Lone Birch and yet the majority of Harper High's staff are there. They are curious about the process and the feedback. Recognizing and acknowledging that collaborative school reviews can be perceived as high-stakes for staff, Clay reaffirms that this is about how a school and system learns. He reminds them that collaborative school reviews are not an appraisal. No single class or teacher will be named and the aim is to look for patterns and trends related to the areas of focus using observational data.

Clay explains how the members of the external review team collectively share their observations and together how they build the feedback. Harper High is a solid school; the students are doing well, but he asks if they could do better: What is the pathway to go from good to great? What would that entail? He acknowledges the respectful relationships among staff and students and the evidence of staff sharing in terms of cuing systems, authentic and real-world examples, and explicit feedback. He talks about observing the effective use of technology. Clay mentions the focus on past traditions—from the trophies and plaques in the halls, to the pictures of the student council, the display cases, the posters for colleges and universities, and the student results—and how all contribute to saying that Harper High is a place of learning. He briefly mentions issues of complexity and differentiation and assures staff that specifics and suggestions for improvement will follow in the written report. Clay asks for feedback and questions from the staff. The entire verbal feedback session takes approximately twenty minutes.

Day 1—the first on-site collaborative school review including the verbal feedback component for Lone Birch—is now complete. Completing the written report and preparing for Meadows Middle School are the next items on Clay's agenda. Juan will ensure that Lea is briefed on how the day progressed.

Meadows Middle School

Introduction and Setting the Stage

It's now three weeks since Harper High's review. There is a degree of anxiety and skepticism among Meadows Middle School staff regarding the upcoming onsite visit. Dante, the school's supervisor, reinforces the message that collaborative school reviews are about how staff collectively learn, that no one would be singled out, that they chose the areas of focus, and that ten to fifteen minutes in a classroom can provide meaningful insights to a careful observer. Additionally, he reminds them that all instructional places will be visited and it is not the individual snapshot but rather the collection of snapshots that will form the entire picture. He then shares some articles on instructional rounds and learning walks. A school visit, a slice in time, supplements the evidence summary the school improvement teams prepared. He talks about how the external review team members will collectively debrief and establish some common understandings. Some of the anxiety lessens.

Mel and his team of five, as they are known, arrive to set up early on the morning of the review. They spoke with Annie and created a simple checklist, which the other schools could now use (see Figure 5.2). He and his team also created a school-based package of information for the external review team members and even include a school pen as a memento.

Because Meadows has just under 300 students, the review requires two teams for a total of six. The external review team includes:[1] Clay and Dante, three different elementary principals from the original team that worked on the Harper High review, as well as Annie, the principal from Harper High, who wants to experience the process from a different point of view. One of the elementary principals has a background in ELL and was a system consultant. Clay tried to get the team together prior to the review in a similar fashion to Harper High but several of the external review team members—Dante and two of the three elementary principals—were dealing with emergencies so the initial meeting to review data simply didn't occur.[2] The individual team members reviewed the data independently and conducted questions and answers via e-mail instead.

Conducting the School Review

The team meet at Meadows Middle School at 7:45 a.m. and Clay leads the initial briefing while the external review team meets in a conference room off the main offices. Dante has a key to lock the door when the external review team is not in classes. Because they did not have their pre-onsite visit meeting, they

---

[1]External teams provide an opportunity for system mentorship and succession planning.

[2]Remember to plan systematically but execute flexibly. In any initiative, unexpected challenges will arise. People will be called away for emergencies. The design and planning quadrants allow you to anticipate these challenges.

Figure 5.2   Day of the Onsite Review Checklist

Action	Designate	Accomplished
# of Review Team Members		
Timetable		
Map of the school		
Schedule for the day	Note if there were to be any last minute changes because of illness, absence, field trips, or supply/occasional teachers.	
Badge for identification		
School improvement plan (SIP)		
The self-assessment survey		
Evidence summary		
Copy of the PowerPoint or other relevant information		
School/classroom newsletter(s) or website information		
School awards		
List of clubs, sports teams, and leadership opportunities for students		
Additional information: • Agendas • Events		

agreed to come to Meadows a little earlier. As he did at Harper High, he reviews the data, the evidence summary, and reinforces the protocols and procedures to be used during the day. To give the team some context, Dante talks about his recent meeting with staff and their concerns about the process of the review. Clay mentions that following the meet-and-greet, the external review team will have time to go over the forms and the specifics based on the school's presentation. By 8:10, they are ready to meet the staff of Meadows Middle School in the library, and although classes begin at 8:30, only a few staff show up. That in itself is telling that the staff is not on board with the process.

Clay and Dante introduce the team members and the review team tries to project warmth and interest as they mingle and chat with the few attending staff. Mel and his small team present using PowerPoint and he tells the members of the review team that copies of the PowerPoint are in the folders the school improvement team has prepared for them, so they shouldn't worry about taking notes. Mel begins by reviewing the traditions and past history of Meadows Middle School and the teams, clubs, and other activities and opportunities that are available for students to develop leadership. One of his team members goes over the relevant school statistics: the transient/mobility rates, the economic challenges parents face, the nutrition programs and homework clubs the staff are beginning to put into place, and the current achievement data. Another member of the improvement team shows off the school's new website. Some of the younger staff have created classroom websites and are communicating electronically with parents—the school has a goal of encouraging more parental engagement and communication. The school improvement team talks about the evidence summary and their ongoing professional learning journey and how they are beginning to implement formative assessment, or as introduced in Chapter 4, assessment for learning across departments. A few, namely the social sciences and the arts, have started to use moderated marking, but it is not yet common practice throughout the school.

By 8:50 the group is back in the conference room, and because the presentation ran a little late, their first observations begin at 9:15.[3] Dante speaks about the student achievement data. Where most schools in Lone Birch are improving—some more quickly than others—Meadows Middle School's scores are stalled for writing and declining for mathematics. Even more worrisome, the achievement gap between males and females is increasing. Meadows Middle School's males are underachieving and increasing numbers of males are being identified with IEPs at the school. These students are being streamed in high school into less academic programs, which impacts their graduation rates and life opportunities. Dante muses, is it a question of requiring special education programs and services or disengaged males with programming not designed to meet their needs? Is it an issue of compliance and not engagement? Issues regarding differentiation are noted in the school's evidence summary. Gender will be an area that the external review team will pay attention to in their classroom observations. In Lone Birch, 60 percent of all identified students are male but at Meadows Middle School the number is approaching 75 percent. As is the case with Harper High, the issue of underachieving male students is compounded by challenges faced by ELL.

The staff in the evidence summary has noted that they have high expectations for their students and feel many of the current students don't or can't meet their high expectations. Mel and Clay want the external review team to see if they observe those high expectations for students using the examples provided from the school's own evidence summary. What is provided when students are not succeeding? What do interventions and accommodations look like in the classroom? Another area they want feedback on

---

[3]Sometimes the timing will be off and the day starts late. Remember to be flexible and you can adjust the schedule during the day by shortening a debriefing session.

is assessment for learning. How is student work being used to provide data for teachers to adjust the student learning? This links to questioning and Clay asks the team to consider who is asking the questions and who is answering. Do they probe for understanding or is the intent recall? For the first three classroom observations,[4] Clay, Dante, and Annie each take one of the elementary principals. The school is small and armed with maps; the review team thus begins their observations. At Harper High, teachers left their doors open for the review team, but here most classroom doors are closed. After the first three observations, the members are back and Clay leads the thirty minutes for deconstruction.

The review team shares that in the initial observations, they mainly saw traditional teaching, with students seated in rows.[5] Only in one class were the students working in groups, and in another, although students were seated in clusters, they were working independently. In two of the initial six classes observed, there were anchor charts and exemplars posted, and these were for the subjects where teachers were beginning to use moderated marking. The questions and tasks were at the knowledge and comprehension level; the question wait/response time was short—only one to three seconds. Several members of the external review team mention that it was difficult to talk with students in conversation during the teacher-directed class time. There were a few indicators that assessment for learning was being used. A few students shared a teacher-created rubric they use to complete the assigned task with the review team members, others talked about handing in drafts of writing before the final paper was due, and the review team members noted the posted cuing systems in the two classes. None of the indicators for high expectations staff suggested were evident in the first set of observations; however it is still early in the day.

By approximately 11:30, the team returns from their next round of four classes. This debrief session combines with a working lunch so the team chats and eats. Clay probes: What are the look-fors for high expectations? Do teachers believe their students are capable and can meet the high expectations? Was student learning and thinking visible in classrooms? What is similar and what is different from the first set of observations? Again the dominant instructional strategy was teacher-led classrooms using a lecture or question format, or having students quietly and individually take notes from textbooks. It was evident only part of the class was paying attention and the members of the external review team note that the students in the back were mainly males who appeared bored and disengaged. Students, if working independently, answered questions from the text or were copying teacher-written notes from the board. Again the wait time was short and the questions and tasks focused on knowledge and recall.

---

[4]In terms of the makeup of the teams, whenever possible, have an experienced member partnered with someone with little or no experience so that a coaching scenario is set into place. This assists with the distribution of learning across the system.

[5]Remember just because students are clustered in groups, it doesn't mean that cooperative learning is practiced.

One of the review team principals talks about "the lack of student voice." Some of the students copying notes didn't understand the material when members of the team questioned them. This leads to a conversation on how, exactly, do teachers check for understanding. Raising this as an issue could provoke discussions among Meadows Middle staff. Many members of the external team comment on the amount of note-taking from the board or from texts.[6] One of the principals mentions her teachers are using a new way to train students in summarizing and note-taking, adapted from *Classroom Instruction That Works* by Dean, Hubbell, Pitler, and Stone (2012). Based on a specific framework, students use bullets for the key points, and create their own visual that reminds them about the key points; then they tweet using 140 characters to frame the main idea.

Another suggestion for Meadows Middle School staff to consider is to ask fewer but more open-ended questions and have students discuss the question and possible answers in small groups with a focus on "accountable talk" because in most classrooms either the teacher spoke or students were working quietly at their desk. The differences between some classroom practices were evident. A few teachers were onboard with the district initiatives and trying new strategies, and yet in many classrooms, it appeared that little had changed. The walls were mainly bare with few posted learning goals or success criteria and textbooks appeared to drive the curriculum.

The next three sets of classroom observations confirm what the review team saw in the earlier rounds. In music and in physical education and a few science classes, students appear more engaged in the activity, especially the boys; however in most classrooms students appear passively compliant and several look bored. The library has a few graphic novels and no real displays to interest students in reading or writing. Dante shares that the school library has the lowest circulation rate per student in Lone Birch. One principal says that he went to Meadows Middle as a student and nothing much appears to have changed.

Debriefing and Sharing Findings and Feedback

As at Harper High, the debriefing and feedback session consists of three activities: the review team's preparation to share its findings and feedback, the debriefing with the school administration team, and the meeting with all staff.

The external review team talks about the issues inherent in changing culture in a school where the staff have been there a long time: How do you engage a staff so they become curious about their own taken-for-granted practice? This is the challenge for the review team. Clay makes note of all of this.

Each member of the review team shares their two areas of feedback for staff. Most suggest ways to move students from disengagement and compliance toward engagement. These suggestion lie on the following areas:

---

[6]Try and be as specific as possible in recommendations for the school under review. Where possible, ground the recommendations in evidence-based practice.

- Student voice. They recommend more student voice and ownership in their learning including the selection of topics under discussion, books, and resources. They want students as more than passive consumers of the curriculum and suggest the school try more cocreated learning, especially learning goals, success criteria, and cooperative group structures. The external review team did not see the effective use of technology and suggests that an increased use of technology might be a way to increase engagement.

- Complexity. The team did not see evidence of high expectations and suggests building staff's capacity to ask more open-ended questions, allow longer wait time, and intentionally build more complexity and rich tasks into the curriculum. This could lead to more accountable talk and more triggers for student thinking to move beyond rote learning.

- Special needs. Concerning meeting students' needs, for ELL, the students need assistance in building their academic vocabulary because many, when asked by members of the external review team, didn't understand or comprehend the words, concepts, or tasks. In addition, there needs to be some gendered interventions to engage struggling disengaged boys. The whole issue of who was identified and why also needs to be brought to the table so staff can use assessment for learning and share strategies to assist struggling students. This is an area where Lone Birch has expertise and central office consultants could be useful.

- Coherence. The team wants to increase the coherence among and between classrooms instead of, as one principal described, "islands of excellence" in a traditional sea.

- Capacity building. They suggest targeted capacity building, aligned to their recommendations, available in the school to encourage regular and intentional use of formative assessment and descriptive feedback, especially for the struggling students. Lone Birch has some system staff who can provide the sessions and the hands-on follow-up.

All of this means that the school's improvement plan would have to be revisited and revised.

An important consideration for the external review team is how they are going to honestly reflect back these findings, both in the verbal and written feedback, without further alienating the staff. Dante suggests a strategy whereby they list what the staff had indicated the team would see in the evidence summary and then mirror back what they actually observed during the various classroom observations. Mel originally suggested this because he wants staff to see the gap between the aspiration and reality on the ground. All of these will involve capacity building for Meadows Middle staff: Where will they begin? What will staff see as their main priority?[7]

Clay says he will add the research and some challenging open-ended questions to provoke courageous discussion, such as the following:

---

[7]These are all questions you can use with your staff to reflect on their practices.

- What is the difference between high expectations and high standards and what are the indicators for each?
- What should be the balance between teacher-led, student work and cocreated learning? Why?
- What are the criteria or things teachers consider when they think about grouping students? When is it appropriate for heterogeneous groupings and when for homogeneous groupings, and why? When should students choose their group partners and when should it be teachers' choice? How do teachers check for understanding that the individuals in the groups are learning?
- When students copy notes from the board or lectures, how do teachers check for understanding? What questions do they ask? How do they decide when they have to loop back and reteach a concept or skill and when is it time to move on?
- What purposes do the current worksheets serve? If Meadows Middle is committed to a climate of high expectations, how can the tasks become more complex?

The external review team meets with Mel, the same way they had with Annie at Harper High to offer a more thoughtful and specific debriefing. Mel isn't surprised: it is what he observes on a daily basis. He looks forward to the written report as a lever for change at Meadows Middle School. He says, "It will be a refreshing dose of reality for some staff." He and Dante will meet to discuss options for unpacking the written report. The external team is now prepared for the verbal feedback session.

The whole-staff verbal feedback session at the end of the day parallels the one at Harper High. This time, all members of the review team stay to provide solidarity to Clay and Dante. Unlike the morning session, this time most of the staff come to hear what the review team will say. Clay acknowledges that the onsite visit and review process can be perceived as high-stakes for staff. He reaffirms that collaborative school reviews provide a tool for learning for both Meadows Middle School and the Lone Birch system. He reminds the staff, again, that collaborative school reviews are not about appraisals. No single class or teacher will be named and the aim is to look for patterns and trends related to the areas of focus using observational data. Clay explains how the external review team collectively shares their observations and together how they scaffold the findings to develop the feedback. The Meadows Middle School improvement team gave the review team a lot of data to examine and analyze and the feedback now is based on impressions, and more descriptive feedback will follow with the written report. Dante talks about how the staff cooperated in developing the evidence and data and acknowledges the contributions of the school improvement teams. Clay mentions that traditions are evident at the school—the athletic plaques, pictures and mementos, and the honor rolls celebrating student success. Clay talks about the recent acquisition of technology and how, when it is used, the review team observed greater involvement of students. He asks some of the questions he and the members of the external review team had created earlier.

Then he asks for feedback from staff about the day and the process. One teacher quietly asks Clay for feedback on her teaching—Clay explains that this is not part of the process. Feedback for appraisals are part of the performance review protocols. Another wants to know how the review team could make decisions based on such short observations. Clay talks about layering classroom data and how all classrooms were visited. Another teacher asks what will happen with the recommendations. Clay reiterates that the staff will take the suggestions into consideration and together as a staff with Juan they will shape their response. For Clay, there is another review report to write and one last school preparing for its review.

Pleasant Valley Public School

Introduction and Setting the Stage

Two of three collaborative school reviews are now complete and it is time to prepare for Pleasant Valley. The staff worked together on the preparations for the review, as discussed in Chapter 4, and they are excited but nervous to show the review team what positive changes have occurred at their school. They created their evidence summary with input from the entire staff. Jill notes that as staff begin to realize gains, even small gains, it increases their commitment to and ownership of improvement. Jill is committed to team learning.

The Pleasant Valley staff created a video clip as their presentation for the external review team. It contains clips of some of their successful activities, student assemblies, and staff talking about key points in the school's improvement plan. One teacher checks that the equipment is working and the video clip is cued. Jill is a visible hands-on principal. She regularly and purposefully visits classrooms and uses her observations to measure progress against the school improvement plan and to involve the staff in discussions regarding the data. She understands that high visibility in classrooms is key to being an effective instructional leader. Jill recognizes that managing crisis from her office will not result in a high-achieving school. Like Annie, Jill works hard to share responsibility and build her leadership team.

She uses the template that Mel prepared to gather a package for the review team including the following:

- A DVD copy of the presentation
- A timetable for the external review teams
- A map of the school, and for each team their classes are highlighted so they know the rooms they will be visiting
- School newsletters, some of which had been translated into different languages
- The latest eco-award
- A list of all the school teams and clubs including a Mandarin, chess, and Spanish club
- The results from the self-assessment survey

- Examples of some assessments for learning and how they were used in moderated practice sessions, where teachers brought the assessment and samples of students' work, and then discussed how they were assessed and how the evidence from the assessment would change or reinforce their practice
- The results from the latest parental survey
- A list of the school's community partners
- The evidence summary staff had created for the school review

This external review team is composed of eight members on four teams. Clay has several members on this team who were on the previous reviews. The consultants for special education and for ELL form part of the team given the specific types of programs found at Pleasant Valley. This time the instructions for the external review team go more quickly. As always, Clay ensures that the team is composed of experienced reviewers and those with little or no experience because he has come to understand that building the capacity of administrators on the review team is part of the collaborative school review process. The external review team met in advance as they had done with Harper High to discuss the evidence summary. Jill's team had also listed in advance the multiple data sets they use to monitor progress with the current results and trend data from the major data sets.

Conducting the School Review

The day of the onsite visit arrives. The external review team arrives at the school by 8:00 a.m. There was one emergency, as one of the members had fallen and hurt her leg and is limping with a cane. Thankfully, anticipating such incidents, Lone Birch has a list of "supply external reviewers" and a new member of the team arrives on time. Planning matters! Pleasant Valley is tight for space and the library was booked well in advance of the onsite visit for a presentation by the community police. The only dedicated and secure space that could be freed up is the staff room, which is an imposition. The team will thus eat their lunch in Jill's office so staff can relax, but the staff room will otherwise be out-of-bounds for most of the day. Dante briefs the new member of the team and Clay chats with the other members of the external review team regarding the submitted evidence summary.

By 8:20, the external review team is ready for the meet-and-greet in the library. Clay, Dante, and the team introduce themselves. Jill begins her introductions, hands out copies of the package they prepared, and then her team takes over. Teachers who can stay for the presentation are welcome but most have classes to teach. As the video clip is played, different staff comment on sections of the video, which emphasize the focus on improvement, supporting student leadership, and engaging parents and the community. Other members of the team talk about the various resources in the prepared package. Staff are invested in the review process.

Just before 9:00, the external team are back in the Pleasant Valley staff room. Clay remarks how different each school's presentation has been and what it says about the climate and culture at each school. Dante reminds the team that the school is situated in a vulnerable neighborhood and shares that given the low socioeconomic backgrounds of many students and the number of ELL, Jill and her staff know it is important to encourage student voice. So staff ensure the students spend time in small groups and in pairs or triads discussing their reading and writing to build their vocabulary and comprehension—oral language competencies, accountable talk, and student voice matter for ELL. Hopefully the team will see lots of students working in small groups, teachers using culturally relevant examples, and the use of other high-yield strategies across classrooms.

By 9:15, they are in their teams and out in classrooms. Clay and the team in their first four classroom observations note the consistency in the anchor charts, learning goals, and messaging. As indicated on the evidence summary, the external team members see a balance of teacher-directed and small-group instruction. Students are working effectively and respectfully in groups. It is the literacy block so they also see an example of guided reading, interactive read-alouds, and some shared writing activities (Pinnell & Fountas, 2011). Teachers try to ensure that students know what they are learning and how the specifics connect to the larger concepts and skills. The learning goal is posted in every classroom. Some members of the team note that there is less technology available in the classrooms than in their more affluent schools. Most classrooms have posted word walls that blend high-frequency words with academic vocabulary to build comprehension as a cuing system for students, especially the ELL. Some have separate math or science word walls. There are lots of cocreated anchor charts and exemplars strategically placed throughout the rooms. One elementary principal remarks how the "walls talk" at Pleasant Valley. The halls are covered with student work alongside posted learning goals and success criteria and rubrics. These are also consistently evident in teachers' classrooms indicating that they are being implemented as whole-school strategies. There are pictures representing student diversity and awards and plaques posted.

During the initial debrief, the members of the review team talk about how they saw evidence mentioned during the presentation. They are excited to see the intentionality in classroom practice and similar practices from class to class such as the posted learning goals from a school that is on the move. It is clear that the teachers are collaborating. One comments that there were no announcements and Dante explains how Jill was firm—literacy blocks had no interruptions. The next set of observations include visual arts, music, and the library/resource room special education as well as the remainder of the literacy block.

The library/resource room has a SMART Board and there is one additional SMART Board for the entire school, which migrates from class to class. Jill received a grant from one of the large bookstores to refresh their collection with more graphic novels and dual-language texts. The teacher librarian visited other high-circulation libraries and is intentional in creating an invitational environment for reluctant readers and writers. In the experiential classes (physical education, art, and music), teachers are very precise in their descriptive feedback.

Given the plethora of special needs and the commitment to inclusion as the first preference, schools today, as Pleasant Valley illustrates, are more complex. The self-contained (congregated) special education classrooms are for students with complex learning problems including autism and a class of medically fragile students, most of whom are tube-fed and nonambulatory or nonverbal. The district has constructed a Snoezelen room for sensory input and as a calming tool when students become agitated. There are multiple adults in these rooms including teaching assistants and child and youth workers working together. A nurse visits the medically fragile students daily to supervise the tube feeding and catheters. The other class has an assigned psychologist who is in one half-day per week and is on call for crisis intervention. Some of those students are runners and unpredictably violent.

Jill ensures these self-contained classes are visited as frequently as the others. She and staff talk about "what is good for some and necessary for all." She and relevant staff including the resource teacher have been gathering data on incidents, attendance, and learning goals, so they shared this with the external review team as part of the evidence summary. In the special education classes and kindergarten classes where there are several adults always present in the room, they talked about the division of roles and responsibilities that honored the skills and knowledge of the staff. In previous reviews, especially for students with learning disabilities, the

Reader Reflections

Issues regarding serving students with special needs are one that we all face in our schools and districts. We have been involved in both district- and provincial-level special education reviews. Some questions to ponder include:

What comprises special education in your district?

What is valued? Why?

Are there inequities in terms of students receiving special education services and programs (e.g., more boys, more students from low SES, more ELL, more students from visible minorities)?

What do accommodations and interventions look like in classrooms?

How do you ensure adults work collaboratively in classrooms serving students with special needs?

What does effective teaching and learning look like in these classrooms?

What evidence is gathered in terms of the effectiveness of interventions used in these classes? What works and how do you know?

review team saw mainly paper-and-pencil tasks and low levels on Bloom's taxonomy. Technology wasn't used effectively and some teachers were teaching as if there were cognitive impairments and not just learning disabilities. It is refreshing to be in classrooms at Pleasant Valley where special education strategies are supportive and intentional. This is an area of interest to Jill.

Debriefing and Sharing Findings and Feedback

The process that follows mirrors the sessions from the two previous schools. By the end of the day, the review team is buzzing. One member saw an activity board based on student choice where students selected how they would represent their findings—visual, poetry, note-taking, a PowerPoint—differentiation in action. Another shares that one of the Grade 2 teachers did an interactive read-aloud using a fairy tale; the students described what made a fairy tale and then were asked to share examples from their own cultures. To provoke discussion, the teacher asked the students, "What was the big idea from the fairy tale?" The kindergarten teacher used inquiry questions at the play centers so students were involved in purposeful exploration: What made the water wheel turn faster? How many blocks could you use before the tower toppled and did it matter what size the blocks were?

Members of the external team comment that the school "walks the talk" of improvement. They observed common practices such as posted learning goals and success criteria across classrooms. There were resources and examples in place that were culturally responsive and respected students' heritage. The school provided structures for uninterrupted literacy blocks. The primary class had pictures of their students demonstrating "good readers" and "active listeners." The books the teachers were reading for interactive read-alouds were culturally responsive. The library had boy-friendly reading materials and books in Mandarin and Spanish, the two dominant languages spoken at home. The team agrees it has been an excellent day.

When the team share the initial findings with Jill as they had for Annie and Mel, Jill is pleased with the feedback. The school appears to be on the right track. Jill mentions a question she frequently asks her staff. She asks them to identify one or two things in their classrooms that they want her to pay attention to that the teachers feel impact their students' learning, and then asks them why. Jill has no preconceived response but uses the question to build intentionality and reflection as staff skills. Several of the participating principals write down this question to use with their own staff. Lea has told the members of the external review team from the beginning that sharing effective ideas and strategies is part of the learning process embedded in collaborative school reviews.

The verbal debrief at the end of the day goes smoothly; Dante speaks first and thanks the school and members of the review team. Clay presents a brief overview and mentions the uninterrupted literacy blocks and some of the common practices observed across classrooms. Once again he asks for feedback and staff share that preparing for the collaborative school review was a lot of work, but worthwhile work. Having visitors in the classrooms wasn't as stressful as they had initially thought, but as one teacher adds, they are glad to get their staff room back. The three pilot reviews for Lone Birch are now complete.

What will the reports say and how will the individual schools and the district unpack these findings? Accountability is the next quadrant for collaborative reviews.

Reader Reflections

If you asked staff to identify one or two things in their rooms that are important, what might they answer?

Is this a type of reflective question you could ask?

What would need to be the preteaching before staff would be comfortable with this type of dialogue?

Thinking Out

In our experience, as the review day progresses and the observational lens becomes more focused, the observations get easier and the conversations and debriefing dig deeper into what is effective learning. It is important to reinforce protocols and keep the external team on track and nonjudgmental because given the constant demands on time, it is easy to become distracted and focus on fixing the teaching and not instead drill deeply into student learning. Ensuring the same process is followed increases interrater reliability and comfort level for the members of the review team. Keeping notes during the day ensures the development of findings are documented, layered, and grounded in evidence. Questioning is important to critical thinking, so the team leader should use prompts to help the external review team unpack their observations and recommendations.

On reviews, we have observed that most educators are not yet clear in terms of what distinguishes students on-task and attentive to the lesson and those who are engaged in their learning. Another area that will require clarification is what constitutes complexity and higher-order thinking in terms of questions and tasks. During reviews, we rarely see or hear rich tasks or questions aimed at increasing complexity in thinking. City, Elmore, Fiarman, and Teitel (2009), in *Instructional Rounds in Education: A Network Approach to Improving Teaching and Learning,* wrote, "When we put teachers and students in situations where the task is vague and unspecified, but the expectations for performance are specific and high, we are expecting them to do the right thing without knowing the right thing to do" (p. 31).

Another area where faculties are trained but not necessarily understanding or internalizing is differentiation in terms of instruction and assessment. Often system-level staff will talk about all of the training sessions they provide, but that is not the same as deep understanding and building expertise. These revelations can be meaningful learning experiences.

Overwhelmingly, administrators and staff tell us that the descriptive feedback is fair. We mirror back, in different words and ways, what staff really already intuitively know. The challenge is to honestly reflect back negative findings, both in the verbal and written feedback, without further alienating the staff.

Some members of the external review team will opt to stay for the debriefing session; some may have other meetings to attend. You may want to add this to the protocols or leave it for the review team members to decide. It is clear however, that if all members of the external review team are there, the messaging is that the process is important.

IN SUMMARY

This chapter has taken you through three different but similar approaches to implementing a collaborative school review. The discussions of the school teams and the external reviews provide models to structure your own review. Four components in the implementation of collaborative school reviews differentiate it from other forms of school reviews: (1) attention to fidelity in the model design, (2) the focus on a collaborative approach, (3) capacity building as an embedded component of the process, and (4) the requirement for a work plan to move forward and the aim to engage staff in building shared understanding and commitment for improvement.

For further information and additional resources, please visit the website associated with this book at www.collaborativeschoolreviews.com.

6 Unpacking the Results

Ensuring Improvement Happens

W e have conceptualized and designed the school review, we have planned how to go about conducting it, and we have followed how three schools went about conducting their school reviews. Now let's look at how to work with the results. What did Lone Birch find out and what can they do about it? This chapter focuses on securing accountability and the four key components related to this function: (1) the accountability structure, (2) analysis, (3) follow-up plan, and (4) monitoring and evaluation of the collaborative school review process.

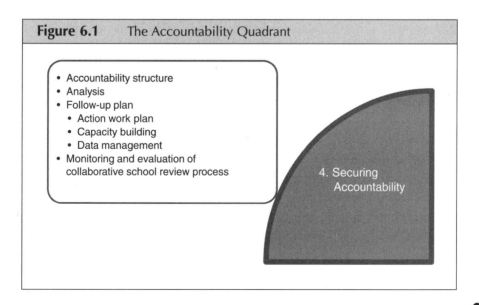

Figure 6.1   The Accountability Quadrant

- Accountability structure
- Analysis
- Follow-up plan
  - Action work plan
  - Capacity building
  - Data management
- Monitoring and evaluation of collaborative school review process

4. Securing Accountability

ACCOUNTABILITY STRUCTURE

Roles and Responsibilities

Collaborative school reviews are a component of a comprehensive performance accountability system. This assumes that the district has the structure and processes in place to monitor and report performance results and to take corrective action. For us this includes completing the following:

- Specify goals, objectives, desired results (outcomes and impacts), and the measures of success that will be used, including the key indicators of success.
- Delineate the data that will be generated, tracked, analyzed, and reported.
- Establish processes and protocols for monitoring, analyzing, and reporting results.
- Establish process for developing corrective action including roles, responsibilities, and accountabilities as well as time lines.
- Provide a clear loop-back system to the design of policy, programs, initiatives, and services that leads to corrective action regarding issues and design flaws.

The accountability structure must clearly define roles, responsibilities, and accountabilities for getting results. The accountability structure for collaborative school reviews must be in sync with what is already in place within the district. If the district's accountability structure has flaws it will be useful to fix these first. Establishing a different accountability structure just for the collaborative school reviews may be a useful exercise if used as a model, but it will not rectify issues at a district level unless this is specifically intended. This must be part of the plan and result in changes that apply to the accountability structures for all other aspects of the district's work. We suggest that in designing the accountability structure for the collaborative school review process, you begin with a review of your current accountability structure to determine where it is and if there is a need for adjustments.

To impact change, the results from the data analysis and onsite observations, along with the suggestions for improvement, must be accepted at the school level and then implemented across schools. Even then, if staff lacks the capacity, resources, and time to make the suggested changes, little systemic improvement will happen. This becomes more important when thinking about implementing complex changes resulting from adoption of the CCSS. Collaborative school reviews are a process for improvement, not an event—the process is still continuing at Lone Birch. In this quadrant, we examine two distinct but inter-related activities that must occur. First, unpacking the findings and feedback contained in the verbal feedback session and written report must occur at the school level and involve all staff. The schools need to collectively review, analyze, and make sense of their individual reports. Second, the analysis must occur at the system level. The district needs to overlay all the individual collaborative school review reports, and then analyze the overall findings to identify patterns, trends, and implications. The district administrators need to isolate systemic issues and challenges, and identify and seize the opportunities for improvement. This is strategic accountability.

Classroom learning is pivotal. To impact classroom learning, the school needs to achieve the following:

- Understand the findings and the suggestions for improvement.
- Identify what is in their control to change.
- Differentiate what can be done immediately or in the short-term and what will require sustained change over time.
- Identify what additional capacity and resources are required to affect change.
- Delineate and develop an action plan for implementing suggestions for improvement:
  o How the school will implement the changes
  o How the school will monitor, evaluate, and report on progress

To support schools, the system needs to do the following:

- Overlay the various written reports to look across the schools.
- Identify patterns, trends, and outliers.
- Identify structural opportunities to better support the schools in achieving the SMART goals. This includes supports to teachers, principals, and vice principals.
- Look for effective strategies currently being implemented in the district that can be transferrable to other schools.
- Identify gaps in implementation in terms of high-yield strategies and targets.
- Identify opportunities for capacity building linked to the gaps.
- Develop suggestions for revisions to the existing processes:
  o District improvement plan
  o Collaborative school review process
- Consider adapting demonstration classrooms or schools where intentional and coherent learning occurs.
- Develop a plan for reporting and sharing the collective findings with board members and other stakeholders and as specified in the particular design of the collaborative school review process.

Verbal Feedback and Formal Report

The verbal feedback is the first stage in the accountability process and intended to mirror back to the school what the external review team observed and their suggestions for improvement. As discussed in Chapter 5, the school supervisor should lead the feedback and if possible all members of the external review team should be present. These sessions give the staff a quick reflection of what the external review team found. The factual data, depth, and analysis reside in the written reports.

The next stage is the formal written reports. In our experience, there is not one format for the written reports that suits all contexts. They should, however, be reasonably consistent across the school district to enable collation and analysis. This means using a proscribed template or limiting responsibility for writing the formal report. Hattie (2012) has indicated the feedback is most powerful when it relates to the existing degree of proficiency, is timely, specific, and clearly demonstrates where improvement is required. Think of the verbal and written reports as a form of descriptive feedback. There may be variance in considerations such as panel. High schools may require a different version of the template than elementary schools. As we have said all along—context matters. The written reports can be as detailed as the district wants; however there are some components which we believe should be standard in your reports:

- *Time lines and identifying factors.* Include the date of the review and the name of the school.
- *The members of the review team.* We suggest indicating the lead reviewer's name.
- *The administration of the school.* You could include the team from the school that worked on the collaborative school review. We have seen just the principal or head teacher's name listed but think of this as an opportunity to build ownership.
- *A section on school context.* This brief overview and description of the school could include: mission, demographic data, areas of involvement or focus, cocurricular activities, parental involvement, and the community or social agency involvement. Often this can be drawn from the school's presentation, website, impressions by the external review team, and input from the supervisors.
- *The areas of focus being examined.* This should include both the district determined and the school-based determined.
- *A data tapestry component.* This should include the relevant student achievement data analyzed:
  o The data must contain multiple measures to create a valid and reliable picture of student achievement.

o The relevant data can be in a summary format, a data narrative, or in a visual format.
o The analysis of data should identify patterns, trends, and outliers.

● *A section containing the evidence summary developed by the school.* This is the summary produced for and used by the external review team.

● *The findings.* Think of descriptive feedback:
  o What the review team saw, heard, and read during the onsite visit—this substantiates what was anticipated, based on the evidence summary or highlights not reflected in the evidence summary. The aim is to mirror back to the school what was seen, read, and heard in a way that makes sense to them and that they can accept to move the findings forward.
  o Suggestions for improvement—in some districts, these may be framed as recommendations. It is essential in a collaborative process that the suggestions center on areas based on the data, analysis, context, and observations and are framed as considerations for staff's use. The research base should be noted so that it can inform practice. The focus needs to be on the priority needs. The strategies suggested should provide a guide to the school on how to move forward with improved learning. It is essential that these align with the data analysis. Specific references in the written report may include: specific programs, texts, websites, or manuals that are evidence-based and can assist the school with implementation of the suggested improvement.
  o Consideration for the school's improvement plan—this should summarize and highlight the main points from the report.
  o Targeted action steps to build on lessons learned.
  o Resources (human and otherwise) to assist with implementing the suggestions for improvement.
  o Suggested time lines for monitoring.

● *Date for upcoming debriefing session.* At that meeting, the school's improvement team will orally deliver the collaborative review report.

● *A summary of the areas suggested for improvement in the collaborative review report.* These are areas the staff collectively agreed to focus on and should be presented as a work plan with key agreements, actions planned, time lines, key milestones, and responsibilities.

We suggest you play with the components for the report to best suit your needs and context: You may want the student achievement data analysis component as a separate section. You may want to blend the suggestions for improvement for the school improvement plan into the section dealing with the indicators. You may want to be more forceful and suggest recommendations for improvement as a heading. Your district must own the written reports and be prepared to use them as change agendas. Make sure they are completed in a timely manner—effective feedback that is timely and specific is the most useful in a change process (Hattie, 2012). It is critical to keep the momentum up and to use the energy and synergy that the review process engenders as a catalyst for the change process. Remember the intent of the whole process is to help staff and administrators understand what was found, to accept the findings, and most critically, to act on the suggestions by incorporating these into their work. Consider a length of five to ten pages. If it is longer, add an executive summary. Too many suggestions for improvement are counterproductive. What will be your and the school's levers of change?

ANALYSIS

Unpacking the Reviews

School Level

As the Lone Birch case study demonstrates, the analysis is organic and occurs at several stages during the collaborative school review process. The first occurs when members of the external review team receive the data and evidence, and then individually or collectively begin to raise questions in terms of what they might see during their onsite visit. We suggest that whenever possible, this step be done collectively to assist the members in developing a shared understanding of what to look for and how to interpret what they see. Remember these are *collaborative* reviews. The second stage occurs onsite at the individual school with the external review team. The analysis at this stage is informal and organic. The team uses both the data tapestry and their observations to tease out possible meaning and trends. Using these observations and the student achievement data prepared by the school, the external review team begins to reflect back what they saw or did not see in terms of the evidence summary. Findings begin to emerge assisted by the team leader's probing questions. These observations lead to the initial development of suggestions for consideration and improvement for the school under review.

Findings from the onsite review and evidence summary data are thoughtfully analyzed so that they can be crafted into a written report. The analysis at this point involves the more formal grouping of the data sets and identifying patterns and trends: Which groups of students are achieving and which are not? What do research and effective practices suggest as areas of focus based on the trends, patterns, and outliers in the achievement data? What are some evidence-informed strategies that could be used as interventions or effective and coherent practices across classrooms? These findings are developed through the onsite conversations but also as the designate for the report as it begins to drill down on the task. This layered process is used to formulate observations and identify strategies and interventions for the school's staff. Included will be those areas that were discussed at the onsite debriefings and which the school staff has agreed to use.

Once written, the school's formal report has to be presented and unpacked at the school level. This is an additional component of the analysis. The administration, the school improvement team, and we strongly urge, the entire staff need to consider the report and begin to develop an action plan to implement the suggestions for improvement that have resonated. They need to also ensure the feedback is timely—if months go by between the onsite visit and the written report, the process has lost its urgency and credibility. Make sure the observations and suggestions for improvement are aligned, descriptive, and based on the evidence summary's focus. The requirement for the schools needs to have two components: sharing the report at the school and developing an action plan to respond to the report. The action plan needs to specify what the school leaders will do to implement the suggested changes, how these will be implemented, who will carry responsibility, and the time lines for each of the actions that will be taken.

District Level

At a district level, you will want a copy of the school plans and a method to periodically monitor their progress. It might be useful to have a regular update on the progress from the school principal linked to the monitoring and reporting of their school's improvement plan and process. This way, collaborative school reviews are aligned and a relevant part of a districtwide accountability cycle.

The next stage of analysis is the more complex district-level analysis. Once all the district reviews for the cycle are complete, the individual school reports need to be layered and analyzed from a system perspective. You will need to go back to the indicators of success—the expectations for results or outcomes that were established for the implementation of the collaborative school review process. These were to be defined as part of the design for the collaborative school review process, as noted in the discussion of the strategic lens in Chapter 1 and the first quadrant in Chapter 2. These desired outcomes should now serve as a lens for identifying the findings that are critical to improvement—not just at a school level but as a whole district. What needs to be pinpointed are those findings that the district needs to act on as a priority.

Based on our experience, the following are some considerations to begin the analysis of the written reports:

● How strong was the evidence summary the schools provided? Was there something of importance overstated or missing? What needs to change?

● Do the findings of the review teams clearly relate back to the evidence summaries? Are there specific examples or data drawn from the focus areas selected by the school? Are the findings well-grounded and documented? Can the school staff see themselves and their students in the report? This is important for collective ownership.

● Do the reports provide a good understanding of the schools? For example, in terms of context and references throughout the report, is there mention of specifics in terms of initiatives and projects the school is working on or unusual clubs or other unique features? Are the student achievement data used to highlight trends and patterns such as boys underachieving in reading and writing, or recent improvements in comprehension?

● Are the suggestions for improvement grounded in research and effective practice? Are they specific with details so the staff at the school can begin to plan for next steps?

● Thinking about issues of confidentiality, is the report depersonalized? Ensure that no specific teacher or staff member is referenced or identified and the report highlights patterns and trends across classrooms

● Is there consistency across the various written collaborative school review reports in terms of language and recommendations? Is there alignment back to the district's improvement plan (DIP)?

The next step is to analyze the data base provided by these reports to tease out the district-level change implications. Questions that you will want to ask include:

● What do the data tell us about our schools and how students are learning?
● What does this mean for us as a system? Is it positive or negative? Are we on the right track?
● What are the common threads?
● What are emerging themes and trends that the data have unearthed?
● What opportunities for improvement have been identified?
● What needs to happen to implement these opportunities?
● What support do schools need for making the changes?
● What are the common blocks?
● What needs to be done at district level to remove these blocks or to facilitate implementation?
● Who needs to take action and responsibility to make change happen?

The value from the collaborative school reviews will come from collectively uncovering, dialoguing, and dealing with any organizational blocks that stand in the way of improvement. This could be in the area of policy, program, capacity, or resource allocation, planning, and accountability structures. The action to be taken should be located in the suggestions for improvement provided by staff and the review teams. Once you have examined the analysis and the opportunities for improvement that have been teased out as requiring districtwide solutions, you will need to establish a system action plan for moving forward. Figure 6.2 provides a district action plan template for your use. We suggest that you use this to document what will be done, how, by whom, and when. This action plan needs to demonstrate your commitment to action and be a useful vehicle to ensure that the implementation of collaborative school reviews results in enhanced organizational capacity and student improvement.

Work Plan to Implement Suggested Changes

The third and essential component of the accountability framework is ensuring that action is taken, based on the findings, to move the school forward. This requires detailed and practical plans for implementing the improvements suggested through the collaborative school review process so that implementation becomes a system priority. Additionally all key stakeholders need to understand and support these plans. The system must be committed to implementation or nothing will change.

As noted in earlier chapters, what we are talking about is continuous improvement to impact learning. Change is the name of the game and this requires that the schools and the district address a follow-up process in a disciplined and focused manner, based on the design, planning, and effective execution of the review. This requires the following: developing an action work plan for the next steps, addressing capacity building based on analysis of possible shortcomings, ongoing data management, monitoring the progress of the changes being implemented, and tracking expected outcomes. The goal in the accountability quadrant is to ensure that the findings from the collaborative school review process will be used both at the school level and system-wide to change teaching practice to positively impact student achievement.

Additionally the findings from the analysis of the collective reviews need to tie back to the first quadrant as a means of validating the currency and efficacy of the design of the collaborative school review as an effective change instrument for the district. Findings should be analyzed for indications of needs for adjustments to the collaborative school review policy and processes to ensure that it is yielding maximum benefit.

We acknowledge that setbacks and challenges to improvement will occur. Leaders at a school and system level must be intentional on how to interpret and deal with setbacks. If the communication is negative, then

Figure 6.2 District Action Plan Template for Addressing Results of the Collaborative School Reviews

Key Findings	Implications	Changes Required	Action Plan	Resources	Time Lines	Responsibility	Monitoring Plan

Key findings. Those conclusions derived from the analysis of the collective collaborative school reviews that have meaning for the whole district and which require a district-level response. The indicators of success—the expected results or outcomes—would have been defined in the first quadrant as part of the design for the collaborative school review process and these should now serve as a lens for identifying the findings that are critical to improvement at a district level.

Implications. What the findings mean for the design of district policies or programs, or for district planning. The implications should address both the short- and the long-term requirements.

Changes required. The critical changes the district needs to make as a whole to fix the problems identified in the collective analysis of the reviews conducted at each school. These should be specific and doable. The changes need to be clearly defined so that administrators, staff, parents, and stakeholders can understand the reasons and the urgency. These could include:

- Adjustments to policy and programs design, planning processes, implementation procedures, and accountability structures and processes
- Capacity-building initiatives
- Data management
- Communication and reporting

Action plan. The specific steps and action that will be taken to effect the changes identified as being critical. For example, changes to policy and program may require a series of steps such as establishing a review committee, consultation, or the development of options for key changes and approvals. Actions may involve redefinition or clarification of current roles and responsibilities.

Resources. The resources both human and technical required so that the changes can occur.

Time lines. The time frame for the completion of each action.

Responsibility. Identification of who will carry the lead responsibility to ensure action will take place as planned, within the allocated resources and time lines.

Monitoring plan. What will be monitored and tracked, how and when, and how the progress will be reported. As noted in the key findings, the desired results for the collaborative school review should inform the monitoring plan.

improvement will stall. The messaging must be framed optimistically, that with increased effort and focus obstacles can be met. This too forms part of the accountability quadrant. We discuss these three components further throughout this chapter, watching how Lone Birch unpacks the reviews.

Looking In

Unpacking the Reviews at the Schools

Back at Lone Birch, the verbal feedback sessions gave the staff in the three pilot schools a quick reflection of what the external review team found. The real data, depth, and analysis reside in Clay's written reports, which he prepares with input from the external review teams. The reference team created a draft template for Clay to use with the external review teams (see Figure 6.3). It has input from the stakeholders and is one of a series of templates crafted during the planning quadrant.

Clay finds it takes him about one week to write a single collaborative school review report, or about five to seven hours over several days so he could still manage other tasks.[1] Writing in pieces, Clay makes sure to touch base with members of the external review team when there is an ambiguous suggestion or finding. Both supervisors, Dante and Juan, have offices close to Clay so he also drops in for a chat when necessary. Maria has taken over much of his regular system responsibilities, so he dedicates his time to completing this task. Because he is crafting all three reports, the language and references will be consistent. He keeps within the three-week time line outlined in the initial design.

Clay envisions that if collaborative school reviews are scaled up at Lone Birch, the system will require more than one lead or he will need to have no other duties.[2] The first report takes the longest time and while he has written many reports as part of his current role, much rides on how it is crafted and received.

Within three weeks of the initial onsite visit, Clay and either Dante or Juan will meet with the administration of each pilot school and their improvement team to receive the written report. Built into the design is a reward for agreeing to pilot collaborative school reviews, in the form of a $1,000 designated seed funding for each school to use for release time to assist with unpacking the report and implementing change. This was one of the design features in terms of resourcing costs as a result of implementing collaborative school reviews. Lea had received this advice from Curtis, a superintendent in another school district that implemented collaborative

---

[1] In terms of financial and human costs, the writing still allows the lead to be involved in other projects.

[2] Having a dedicated staff is a major financial and human consideration not viable for most districts. It makes more sense for most districts to have this added as part of an existing portfolio and balance the time per role.

Figure 6.3   Lone Birch Report Template

Date of the review	School name and address
Administration	Review team members
Date of the formal debriefing session	School supervisor

Context:

The review team's impression of the school being reviewed:

Mission, student size, grades or panel, sociodemographics of the students and community, distinguishing features or programs, partnerships, environment of the school, technology, etc.:

What the school wants to recognize and celebrate:

Key Areas

1.

2.

Focus areas for feedback:

3.

4.

Data analysis for the school:

Evidence Summary and Relevant Data	What the Review Team Noted	Suggestions for Improvement	Action Steps by School for Improvement
Focus Area 1			
Focus Area 2			
Focus Area 3			
Focus Area 4			
School improvement plan			

Additional comments:
(What will we do as a school regarding our selected focus areas, based on the report? Who will be involved? What tools/support do we need?)

school reviews. Curtis's advice was that if possible, access to seed money for specifics such as release time would help to implement and unpack the school-level suggestions. His district did not do this and there were issues of schools not following through with the suggestions for improvement and thus achievement did not increase.

Harper High School

The schools receive their reports in different ways. Once Juan and Clay have met with Annie and her improvement team, the consensus is to present the report as it was written to all staff at the next staff meeting. Clay and Juan attend this afterschool meeting to answer any questions. Annie strongly urges all staff members to attend and virtually all staff do (with exceptions for family emergencies, which are usually inevitable). Staff group in cross-department teams at tables equipped with markers, one laptop, and enough copies of the highlights from the written report for everyone. Clay and Dante outline the main points, and Dante ends each with the board members' "good to great" theme.

It is quiet in the room. As one teacher said, breaking the silence, "We were hoping it would be more positive." Annie reminds them that the observations were a "slice in time" and that in her instructional walks she sees much the same as is reflected in the written report; this had been shared as feedback to staff at various previous meetings. The school is moving toward critical and complex thinking, but they are not there yet. It also was an area for which staff requested feedback from the team. The findings and suggestions align with the evidence summary that staff developed. The report is complimentary regarding Harper High's current level of achievement but there are possibilities for improvement. Annie reminds staff that continuous improvement is a process and reiterates that the staff now own the collaborative school review report, including the suggestions for improvement. These are not recommendations, but considerations for Harper High to move forward; because they are based on the onsite observations and Harper High School data, they are credible.

Annie then asks staff in their small table groups, what comments in the written report stand out for them? They begin with Clay's questions contained in the report. In their groups, they use colored markers to highlight sections of the reports. Each table discusses the highlights, then summarizes their key points on the laptop using a memory key, and then presents using the SMART Board. There is agreement between Annie and staff: Although Harper High has been working on schoolwide learning, it has not been as consistently implemented as faculty assumed. In particular, the comments about higher-order thinking skills really stand out for Annie and her team. This is something they thought they were doing. The intentional and ongoing use of higher-order thinking skills is an area she previously felt staff needed to focus on if the school was going to move from good to great. The findings relay that the teachers still need to collectively improve their skills and knowledge in this area to move students from where they are to where they potentially could be achieving. Staff agree; however they think they are already using higher-order thinking and are surprised and baffled to realize they are not demonstrating this: What is higher-order thinking? What does it look and sound like?

Increasing rigor and complexity requires the staff to spend time developing their skills and knowledge. This likely will be an area where they use the release time funds provided by the district. It becomes the main component of their work plan arising from the report—it becomes their lever for change.

The improvement team will now take the suggestions and work on some draft action plans for the areas that staff selected as areas for improvement. These will come back to the entire staff for clarification and further discussion. Suggestions in the written report such as cocreating anchor charts, exemplars, and rubrics could be short-term goals. Another short-term goal is to extend wait time and ask more open-ended questions. These short-term goals can be handled internally and the improvement team suggests holding a series of "lunch and learn" sessions and Annie would supply the lunch. She will also ask the Teaching and Learning Department for some texts and resources to use as a basis for these sessions. Differentiation and complexity are longer term goals and to build capacity and sustainability Harper High recognizes that they need to access district-level supports—coaches, materials, and release time.

Some of the actions based on the suggestions in the written report staff select to work on schoolwide include the following:

- Create rich and complex tasks and questions using several cognitive processes at the higher end of Bloom's taxonomy (critical thinking, applying).
  - Promote thinking and reasoning.
  - Have multiple perspectives.
  - Stimulate discussion to encourage students to explore the learning.
  - Build on prior knowledge.
  - Provide alternative solutions or endings.
  - Create analogies.
  - Evaluate—choose among and between answers.
- Build capacity for and use higher-order thinking skills into the school improvement plan across subject areas and grades.
- Create a SMART goal focused on moving more B (Level 3) students to A (Level 4) students.
- Increase staff's ability to differentiate instruction and assessment for students.

Annie and her team begin to prepare a synopsis of the process and share the results for the next parent committee meeting and Harper High's newsletter. It will take the school a while to process all of the findings. The accountability process is just beginning. Juan will be there as he had in the preview meetings to ask probing questions. He will be there for support too, and also to monitor the changes with Annie and make sure that "staff don't wander off practice." Annie will include updates in her blogs, and the action plan arising from the report will become the focus of her instructional walks. Harper High is now moving along the path from good to great.

Meadows Middle School

At Meadows Middle School, in keeping with the Lone Birch process, Clay and Dante give the written report to Mel and his small improvement team. Mel and the team want to ponder it and figure out how they are going to share the results. The improvement team's perception is that many Meadows staff are either cynical or critical of the collaborative school review process. The improvement team wants to focus on using instructional strategies more effectively in more classrooms throughout the school. For examples, the report mentions that in a few classrooms students were working in cooperative group structures and in others individually using worksheets aimed at knowledge or recall. The written report highlights these disparities across classrooms. Mel and Dante agree that a more coherent approach to teaching and learning is required. This is an area that Mel has frequently mentioned in staff meetings, but how to make it happen? They decide to use the existing influence structure in the school, and collectively, they develop a plan: The report will be given to the department heads with the key points marked. One member of the improvement team and the department head will meet with the relevant staff and present the key points and, to get some buy-in, use the commitment of release time.

Thinking of increasing the staff's ability to implement both culturally responsive pedagogy and differentiation including gender-based interventions, the school, with Dante's support, will access system instructional coaches to work with staff. The district will provide some release time for teachers to facilitate the training. Mel is sure that without release time, teachers will not participate in working through the report or attend the additional capacity-building sessions that follow. There is $1,000 allocated for each pilot school, which he will use to buy time for his teachers. Lunch-and-learn sessions operating at Pleasant Valley are not yet an option here.

At the next scheduled staff meeting, once all the departments have met, Dante will present the data to demonstrate how the student body is becoming more diverse and how their needs are similar but also different to previous student bodies. Dante, Mel, and the improvement team will use the existing student data, including the patterns and trends that arose for the analysis, to frame what the review team observed. The staff has not yet made a concerted effort to use student achievement data in a data tapestry to inform their own practice. Mel and the improvement team will emphasize the importance of building collective capacity to support effective learning and meet changing student needs. The focus will be on serving learning needs and Mel knows he must be careful not to appear critical of current teaching practice. Constructive feedback is a balancing act.

To signal a change, rather than working in grade teams or subject teams the way Meadows traditionally has operated, the approach will now be focus-based and schoolwide. Mel and the improvement team resolve that they will share aspects of student data at every meeting and ask the same at the grade- and subject-level meetings. They will use the data to monitor improvement that results from implementing the suggestions in the report. The use of data and the capacity building provided by the district provide a balance between accountability and support. Gathering, aggregating, disaggregating, and presenting data is an area where the system could be helpful initially in ensuring that Mel and his team have the relevant data to share with staff. Mel will also include in his feedback what he observed during his instructional walks that aligns with the suggestions of the written report. Monitoring and reporting back to staff all will form part of their draft work plan and keep them on track toward improvement. Dante promises he will be there for support.

The highlights will be presented in the department meetings and Dante and Mel will share the relevant student data and the changing student needs. These new cross-department and grade teams will coalesce around a few key areas based on suggestions for improvement from the written report:

- Instructional Strategies Committee. Explore what are effective instructional strategies and what characteristics make them impactful. What does research and best practice suggest? The committee will use existing Lone Birch video clips to model what these instructional practices can look like in classrooms. The improvement team wants the grade and subject chairs to benchmark effective practices by visiting other schools to see effective instructional practices in action. The committee will share current research on effective instructional practices. These might be in an other Lone Birch school or in a neighboring school district. For Mel, this is the priority:
  - Work on expanding the use of cooperative group structures.
  - Use more real-world and authentic examples and references so students can see themselves in their learning.
  - Begin to work on making tasks richer and more open-ended.
  - Extend wait time and examine the issue of strategic open-ended questioning.
  - Post learning goals and success criteria and work toward cocreating the learning goals with students.
- Differentiation Committee. Build opportunities for teachers to explore some differentiated instruction into the timetable:
  - Have Lone Birch central staff hold some sessions on differentiation for the range of learners in Meadows Middle classrooms.
  - Look for overarching themes in terms of social justice issues to emphasize equity schoolwide.
  - Begin to engage in moderated marking to develop common language and approaches. Each department will commit to one session of moderating marking per term.
  - Examine boy-friendly resources, strategies, and structures to appeal to the disengaged males using central resource staff.
  - Acquire more graphic novels, informational texts, and dual-language resources to appeal to a range of learners.
  - Using book groups, explore some of the research to meet needs of ELL including developing academic vocabulary and accountable talk.
  - Bring in some speakers from the community to address culturally responsive curriculum.

- Technology Committee. Begin to explore more effective use of existing technology in the school and the acquisition of new technology. This committee will complement and support the work of the other two committees. Technology as a strategy will be used as an enabler for engagement, authentic learning, and assistive technology. This committee builds on recent school directions, as the school is now fully wireless and some funds have been set aside for technology:
  - Complete an inventory of existing technology and existing expertise among staff.
  - Survey students to find out their areas of expertise and interest.
  - Consider consolidating existing laptops in a mobile computing option, so that a bank of laptops can be signed out by a variety of staff to work with students.
  - Train three or four key staff including the teacher librarian on new software using Lone Birch's Technology Department.
  - Visit a neighboring district known for its effective use of technology.
  - Work on improving the school's website and inviting more teachers to create websites with supports.
  - Have Mel begin writing and posting a blog for parents and the community.
  - Look to purchase ten e-tablets that could be used by a class and shared across the school to move toward 21st-century learning. If it is successful, more funds could be forthcoming.

There is a sense that the improvement process designed to improve achievement at Meadows Middle School will require time and ongoing support. Each of the three proposed committees will develop a set of indicators to describe what teaching and learning might look and sound like if the suggestions for improvement are fully implemented. Everyone understands that this is just the beginning of implementation. Once the committee structure is approved, Mel and his team will brief the parent committee and solicit their input. It will be a combination of pressure based on the written report and then expectation for change and support in terms of release time and additional resources, including central office coaches.

Clay and Dante promise Mel that they will be available both for consultation and for regular school visits. They could collectively use instructional walks to look for evidence of implementation based on the suggestions and the work of the three committees. They will monitor the improvement process. On a professional level, Dante promises not to move Mel to another school for five years so he can implement the change at Meadows Middle and follow through with Clay's report. Mel wants change to be clear and transparent, so they will post the committees' agendas on the school's secure website for other staff to see. Mel will also ask staff to monitor and report back as they try these strategies; the feedback from his instructional walks and staff's self-reflection will be used to focus discussions at the staff meetings. He will provide release time for the cross-disciplinary committees and Dante will help. It is the beginning of systemic accountability and improvement for

Meadows Middle School. Mel wonders, as change occurs, what the next collaborative school review will say in five years. He and Dante are cautiously optimistic.

Pleasant Valley

When Clay indicates the report is ready, Clay and Dante debrief Jill and she remarks, "There are no surprises." This is the common sentiment expressed by all three pilot principals. Because the external review team saw evidence during their onsite visit of the areas for focus, Jill knows the staff will be more open to considering the suggestions for improvement. Jill and Dante talked, and given the climate of trust and collaboration at the school, the decision is to jointly debrief the staff. Because Pleasant Valley is the last of the three pilot schools, the buzz is building in Lone Birch regarding collaborative school reviews. For the debriefing, Clay will be invited, but Jill with Dante's help will present the report to her staff.

At the general staff meeting, Dante begins explaining that for Pleasant Valley staff, "The report isn't about changing practice but refining it." He shares that the external review team saw evidence of shared practices focused on improvement. Jill uses Annie's suggestions, based on the Harper High experience, of having staff sit cross-divisionally in tables to encourage small group discussions. Jill asks her staff to sit in these cross-grade teams, explaining that the conversations would be richer. Jill lets staff know that the written report will sit on the internal school's website that only staff can access.[3] She also created a PowerPoint synthesizing the report and each staff member has a copy of this at the table. As is her practice, Jill asks staff to discuss all of the findings and suggestions and decide which they feel will impact learning at Pleasant Valley the most: What would be the key levers?

Each table reports the gist of their conversations using chart paper. Then Jill asks staff at their tables to separate the suggestions for improvement into those that could be completed in the short-term and those requiring longer time lines to explore and implement. She reminds them that all of this must relate back to the Pleasant Valley improvement plan: "This is part of the school's journey—the report is not the destination." The important piece to remember is that they all will have input and share responsibility for changes that occur arising from the report.

Several tables note that there are areas of ensuring equity the staff want to explore further—gender, special education, and ELL. They thought they were making some progress but that the practices of differentiation and timely and tiered interventions still do not go deep enough. Others feel that if they select a focus such as greater emphasis on assessment for learning and descriptive feedback, then they could fold equity into their practices. They would include descriptive feedback into their practice and look for ways to be more effective with cocreating success criteria and rubrics. These are

---

[3]Debriefings should reflect the school's culture and practices and need not follow a common format. We have provided three different models across the pilot schools to consider.

all highlighted as suggestions in the written report and will form Pleasant Valley's draft action plan.

Staff at Pleasant Valley are already using student achievement data and moderated marking to inform their practice, and working on coherent instructional practices among and between classrooms and grades. There is a shared understanding of learning goals and success criteria, and the report highlights that they now need to involve students more in the process of cocreating learning. This is the next level of informed practice for the staff. Discussion occurs at the tables: What is feedback? What makes it effective? These questions form the beginnings of a collaborative inquiry for their learning teams.

Staff decide that they will continue with the work using moderated marking and move toward, as the external review team suggested, more "moderated practice." At their tables, the Pleasant Valley teachers discuss the following:

Short-Term

- Continue to use student data to plan, identify underperforming students, and target interventions. The intent here is to analyze the data on student achievement and to tease out issues and problems. The goal is to understand why students underachieve and to develop strategies to assist them that are targeted and research-based. This will ensure that students will get the help they need to reach their potential. Continue to create and post learning goals with verbs that are action-specific. The change is to have the learning goals more cocreated and less teacher-created as the report suggested. Continue to post rubrics and success criteria but these too should solicit student voice and be cocreated to build in more accountability for their learning.
  - As a whole staff, identify the academic vocabulary (e.g., infer, justify, expand, similarities) that students will need to be successful and work to build these into lesson plans. Decide which vocabulary will be introduced in which grades and which grades will reinforce the vocabulary.
  - Continue to build reading collections in the library and classrooms. These should include boy-friendly, culturally responsive, and, where appropriate, dual-language texts.

Long-Term

- To support student voice and engagement.
  - With Lone Birch support, begin to acquire mobile computing labs and other technologies. Money is tight; Pleasant Valley parents could not raise funds like Harper High's parent council could. They will thus develop a technology plan requiring central supports. They will also look for grants to support this initiative.
  - Explore the issue of strategic questioning as a staff. They will try to build in longer wait time and ask more open-ended questions, as well as more complex questions once they have a clearer idea of

exactly what that sounds like and looks like. A cross-grade committee will be created to develop readings on and examples of strategic
questioning.

o Include more rich tasks to encourage student thinking.

o Create a staff book group to explore the needs of ELL and multi-
literacy. Group will identify effective strategies to use to increase
student voice, understanding, confidence, and comprehension.

• Increase the use of a variety of assessment tools and methods. Staff
will discuss which ones are being used and which ones appear to be
used less. They will also allow students more choice, not only in the
topic but also in how they want to demonstrate their learning.

o Work on increasing the use of assessment for learning and how to
use the data to impact teaching practice across grades and divisions.

o Give students more opportunities to review their work, have peer
feedback, and revise their work before it is marked.

o Refine their practice in terms of descriptive feedback.

o Have the students begin to provide some descriptive self-assessment.

Pulling Out District-Level Trends and Patterns

At a system level, it's about the identification and resolution of systemic issues and the building of approaches that move the whole district
forward. The issue is to identify possible obstacles or blocks to improved
practice: what needs to be addressed in policy and the direction and supports that are provided to schools. The collaborative nature of the collaborative school review process allows the district a unique opportunity
to understand what it needs to do systemically to address blocks to excellent teaching, and identify ways to remove those blocks and introduce
improvements.

As a system, what must be teased out are the areas of strength and needs
that the analysis of the collective collaborative school review data provides:
What is working, and where is progress occurring? What are alignment
issues and what schools are outliers? Which schools are improving, which
are stalled, and which are declining along the improvement continuum? If
the district is organized around families of schools, what patterns emerge?
Does socioeconomic status determine success in achievement? Where are
the achievement gaps? We noticed from Lone Birch some common issues
such as the use of strategic questioning, differentiation, and assessment for
learning. Also there were some common areas of focus for the school-based
action plans such as gender-specific interventions, more cogenerated learning,

and the creation of academic vocabulary. These could be developed across schools to promote shared learning. In your district, there will be commonalities that emerge from the reports and the action plans that can be used at a school as well as the district level.

Additionally, what will be the human and financial costs arising from the recommendations? In difficult fiscal times, this may require a reprioritization of initiatives and strategies. What will impact student achievement the most? Also not everything can be done immediately. Separate short-term and long-term directions and relay these distinctions in the action plan. Can external grants provide some flexibility with moving ahead? These all become considerations.

As we noted in the introduction, there is a sense of urgency to school improvement. There is not one single practice or policy that can turn districts and schools around. As we have maintained throughout this resource, one size does not fit all—change is dependent on context, community, culture, capacity, and resourcing. One sure thing is that it must be a systemic approach from both bottom-up and top-down simultaneously. The individual components have to align and interact synergistically. Collaborative school reviews can assist you to position your school and district along the continuum of change.

It's all about learning at the system and school level.

We have looked at how the three pilot schools received their reports and how they unpacked them and began to proceed to consider and then implement the suggestions for change. So what did Clay and the team actual find and recommend for the three pilot Lone Birch Schools? This is what he reported to Lea and the senior team.

What were the main commonalities across the three Lone Birch School Reviews?

 Looking In

Context

In the context section in all three reports, the external review teams note that the schools are well-maintained and inviting, with the issues of safety and security for visitors explicit. This is part of the Lone Birch safe-and-secure-schools initiative, so the senior team and the board members are pleased about the evidence. There are brochures and messages posted for parents and the community, and Pleasant Valley has a community worker onsite to assist parents and the community. In diverse communities like Pleasant Valley and

Meadows Middle serve, communication to parents goes home in several languages. The district's website posts messages for parents in several languages. Two of the three schools have dual-language texts in their library. Being more effective in communicating to parents and the community is one of the district goals.

In their observations, most students were on-task. Students were not in the halls but in classes focused on their work. There was some variance school to school, with Meadows Middle students least attentive. Relationships between staff and students appear for the most part to be respectful. There are a variety of leadership opportunities in all three schools for students ranging from athletics to clubs with areas of focus including robotics, band, choir, chess, environment, tutoring, and student government, to name a few. In the halls at all three schools, there are mementos, banners, pictures of past graduates, and students on the honor role with key messages celebrating student success and traditions. Harper High refers to this as their "hall of fame." There is also student work posted on walls and halls, with the most at Pleasant Valley and the least at Harper High. In a few instances, learning goals and rubrics or success criteria are posted next to the student work. All three schools have websites with current information. Some are more interactive than others. There is some evidence of teachers' individual classroom websites where they post homework, assignments, field trips, and other notices and some teachers, especially in the middle and high school, are developing blogs.

The Use of Data

The good news is that all three schools referenced the use of student data in their evidence summary. However, because each school review looked at a different division (elementary, middle, and high school), it is difficult to make definitive statements about the effective use of specific tools such as the Kindergarten Developmental Surveys (KDS) used to measure school readiness across schools. While Pleasant Valley appears to be using the results to inform areas of focus in the kindergarten program and areas of support required by families of students in these programs, Lone Birch needs to know, as a system, what else would be required at a district level to ensure the effective gathering, analysis, and use of these data. Some findings are interesting. The focused interventions on literacy in Grades 1–5 appear to impact student achievement as students progress, based on the progression in mastery from primary through the junior grades. Students who scored low on the KDS made substantial gains. This is one school among many. Lone Birch needs to understand if these interventions are influencing achievement across other elementary schools.

Data indicate a focused and coordinated schoolwide literacy strategy in place in both the elementary and secondary school. This means that there are structure supports in place—timetabling, resources, and professional learning. Both the elementary and secondary schools have accessed system literacy coaches. There is little evidence of a coordinated literacy strategy at Meadows Middle School but it will be in their draft action work plan.

In all three schools, gendered achievement results are noted. The young men across all three schools appear to be underachieving in reading and writing, with this most evident at Meadows Middle. The extent of the gap varies across the three schools and is most pronounced at Meadows. There are a smaller percentage of males at the top levels of achievement than females except for mathematics on the main assessments. In the student survey data, most males perceive themselves as good readers and writers despite their lower marks. Fewer boys report using strategies to check their work. This appears to be similar from the junior grades through high school. Yet, the review team found some evidence of gendered interventions in all three schools. In schools with high ELL populations, most of the underachieving males are also ELL. The libraries all have graphic novels and informational texts to appeal to a range of readers, but these were not reflected in most classrooms. Novels and more traditional reading materials were prevalent in classrooms. Pleasant Valley uses leveled texts and organized classroom reading materials by levels and by interests. The implementation of technology across the three schools is uneven.

Another common observation was that most classroom computers were not in use during the instructional day. Computers were a preferred modality for boys. Will this pattern be similar across schools in Lone Birch? How can their existing technology be used more effectively? What are the implications for future purchases?

Instructional Practices

Hattie (2009, 2012); that the differences among and between classes in a single school are sometimes greater than the differences among and between classes in different schools. This appears to be true for Lone Birch too. Despite what Lea and her team thought were clear directions regarding the use of effective strategies, the external review members observed teachers making individual decisions in terms of how they taught and what strategies and approaches they selected to use. The privatization of classrooms was more prevalent than the senior team had benefited. Lone Birch thought they were guiding improved instructional practice, yet the review team observed, in some classes, the intentional use of math manipulatives, open-ended questioning, and cooperative groupings; however most of the classes observed were teacher-led and teachers' voices dominated. Was that because teachers assumed the team wanted to see them teach and that is how they interpreted teaching? Some teachers were using technology creatively and engaging students in inquiry, while in other classes, low-level worksheets were still being used. There were no apparent common understandings and clear, agreed-upon standards of practice to impact student learning. This has implications for messaging, monitoring, and capacity building as a system.

Most questioning of the tasks students were working on was aimed at the lower level of Bloom's taxonomy. This was true across all three schools, though less evident at the high school, which had been working on increasing complexity in student learning, and least evident at the middle school. Wait time between the question asked and the student response was short (less than four seconds) and if the student answered wrong, the teacher moved quickly to the next student. Student voice, whereby students were asked to purposefully discuss among themselves the learning goals and ways to approach the tasks the teacher was using, was most evident at the elementary school. At Pleasant Valley was also the greatest intentional use of group work. At Meadows Middle, students were sitting in table groups but working independently. Cooperative group strategies were not evident in the classroom.

Although Lone Birch had been working on differentiation as a districtwide strategy, the review team observed little evidence. Most students were working on the same task or assignment. Choice was most evident in terms of students selecting the topic, product to demonstrate the task, or in their choice of students to work with or books to read. Teachers had been exposed to staff learning on differentiation but many were still at the awareness stage. In some classes, it was being implemented effectively and the tasks and the assessments were being differentiated to respond to the range of student needs.

Relationships and Trust

In two of the three schools there are supportive relationships between administration and staff. At Meadows Middle, many of the staff have not yet bought into the change agenda and there is less trust and collaboration. For Pleasant Valley and Harper High, the strategies they as a staff are working on have resulted in improved achievement. According to the school supervisors, this increased their sense of self- and collective efficacy. All three schools have evidence of parent involvement and try to reach out to their communities. The schools with greater needs have sought out partnerships with agencies in their community. Two schools are on the continuum of better than the average to good, but no school is truly great. There was evidence of school-based and system professional learning to build capacity, yet it isn't always a collaborative practice. The good news is that all three principals see themselves as instructional leaders and although their approaches and areas of emphasis differ, they are all purposefully visible in classrooms and are monitoring the implementation of their school improvement plan.

It is agreed that the Teaching and Learning Department will use the trends and patterns to review their current training packages, and revise their approaches to how they are delivering capacity building. Some of what the system coaches and trainers have been working on as a district did not appear to be evident in these first three reviews. They as a team will revisit the capacity building and messaging.

The district analysis will raise some interesting questions for Lea and her team: What else is required in terms of providing supportive environments at a system level to support classroom change? They decide it is likely that Lone Birch is working on too many initiatives at once. Lea and her team wonder if the time lines are manageable and the resourcing appropriate: Are the school goals really aligned with the system ones? Is the current approach to professional learning effectively aligned with the system initiatives? Does it allow repeated opportunities for teachers and administrators to further their expertise? Are there sufficient system structures in place to encourage collaboration and coherency among and between schools? To rethink the training and have less districtwide sessions and more at the school level, do they need some model or demonstration classrooms?

These patterns generate discussion among the senior team. Initially there is a sense of frustration—descriptive feedback and effective instructional strategies especially in terms of literacy were system initiatives. They therefore anticipated seeing more coherent practice. Quickly though Lea moves them on to what they will do about these results: What have they learned? Offering professional learning sessions is not the same as ensuring coherent practice. They need to reexamine how capacity building is delivered and monitored in Lone Birch. They need to be more intentional and specific about classroom observations during instructional walks.

Lessons Learned From the Process

As you unpack and layer the results in your district and school, similar patterns will emerge. Implementation is on a continuum and it takes time to reach embedded practice. Often we see superficial and sporadic implementation of effective strategies because teachers lack a model to build on, professional learning has been episodic, and they lack descriptive feedback and opportunities for moderated practice. Lessons learned from the reviews are opportunities to move forward: From the findings, what are the key levers for increasing student achievement? Develop success criteria or indicators of success for these key levers: What will coherent and sustained implementation look and sound like? Focus your efforts and resources strategically on these key levers as well. Celebrate what is already effective, create action plans, and monitor the next steps.

 Looking In

Suggestions for Improvement Across the Three Pilot Schools

The following are some of the types of suggestions for improvement that Clay references across the reports. The language and examples vary but there are some common patterns and trends across the schools:

- Improve the use of student assessment data. Lone Birch teachers and administrators are not yet data-literate and data are not consistently informing instruction and assessment. Student assessment data can be considered as formative feedback to teachers. It forms part of the data tapestry needed to provide information to inform their practice. Teachers are the most important impact factor on student learning. Intentional, evidence-based, and coherent teaching and assessment can increase achievement. The results raise questions: What is the percentage of assessment of learning compared to assessment for learning? Consider creating models to use as assessment for learning by grade, division, or departments. Given that most feedback noted in the onsite visit is timely, corrective, and motivational, look to creating feedback that references the learning goal, acknowledges the ways the student demonstrates the success criteria, and then specify the next steps needed to improve the quality of the student's work. How can teachers expand their repertoire and integrate more higher-order thinking skills? As a staff, consider ways to collaborate to develop and use feedback more effectively. Encourage inquiry-based units using social justice themes and supporting multiple perspectives.

- Increase higher-order thinking skills. In only a few classes, the review team observed the use of complex and critical thinking. Although it is a system goal, it is not happening coherently in classrooms visited. Consider a system and schoolwide emphasis on higher-order thinking in the existing learning teams and departments. Provide professional learning and models for teachers to build upon. Can you incorporate video clips of actual classroom practice? Staff collectively could devise a range of strategic questions, open-ended questions, and starter stems for more complex questions or tasks for students. What distinguishes rich tasks from compliant tasks? How can rich tasks that engage students be created and adopted from the current materials? Consider working collaboratively to increase complexity and richness in tasks to make thinking more visible in classrooms.

- Reconsider the use of worksheets. The review team notes the use of worksheets in many classrooms, supporting the need for richer and more complex tasks. Clay refers to them as "happy, busy work." Consider, as a staff, reviewing existing worksheets to eliminate low-level, commercially prepared worksheets and tasks—that is, spelling words in isolation, grammar, fill-in-the-blanks, word searches, mathematics blackline masters, and photocopied reading series. This will support the development of critical thinking skills. Which worksheets will be kept and which discarded, and why? How as a staff can you collectively (by grade and subject) create more rich tasks to increase complexity? (This suggestion is used in the reports for Meadows Middle and Harper High.)

- Address the dominance of teacher-created materials. The review teams saw a predominance of teacher-bought and individually created materials. The process of cocreation with students emphasizes the "why" of learning. Involve students more intentionally, in the cocreation of rubrics, anchor charts, success criteria, and exemplars to support the feedback loop. Ensure that students have the opportunity to engage in understanding exemplars and what is required to move their own work toward the next level. Lone Birch will centrally have to work on creating models to support teacher learning.

- Improve coherency across classrooms. Most schools had some teachers using effective strategies, data, and descriptive feedback to impact learning, but nowhere near a majority in a school. Emphasize continuing to build collective staff capacity. The coherent and intentional use of high-yield strategies can reinforce students' knowledge and skills. Identify those high-yield strategies that can be used schoolwide and build staff capacity on their use and impact. Develop the use of common language and shared understanding. Consider using collaborative inquiry to increase intentionality and coherency. Consider visiting one another's classrooms as part of moderated practice. Consider expanding the use of moderated marking. (For Pleasant Valley, this is referenced in terms of the effective use of technology.)

- Explore new strategies for English language learners. Teachers' voices dominated during the classroom observations. Consider, as a staff, exploring the research on multiliteracies and the impacts for learning. Consider using more visual and concrete clues and extending wait time (eight to fifteen seconds) so that students can translate, process questions, and use the cues to remember the English words; concepts also may prove helpful. Continue to reference students' culture and experiences. Students need to see themselves reflected in the curriculum. When could students use their own literacies in combination with English? Consider the classroom use of dual-language texts. Have students use their computers, translator, or other smart devices as dictionaries and the thesaurus to expand vocabulary and assist in comprehension. Build in increased opportunities for accountable talk so that students can extend their oral and thinking skills. Consider ways to strengthen student voice in classrooms.

- Extend academic vocabulary and concepts. When questioned, students didn't understand the concepts and directions. The analysis of the high-stakes assessment results indicated this as well. Students didn't understand justify or refute, as well as some of the subject-specific nomenclature. Consider working on a whole-school strategy to intentionally build the students' academic vocabulary to master the understanding—and regular and intentional use—of words such as infer, justify, vertices, deconstruct, and evaluate, as well as the nomenclature that is subject-specific. This will assist students whose maternal language is other than English, those whose parents do not have a high school diploma, and those who do not have books at home. Consider faculty and administrators adapting strategies such as comprehensive word walls, words in context, blogging, tweeting, poetry, and rapping so that students can expand their working vocabulary. These should not be lists of words or spelling lists, but rather students must be able to paraphrase these words to demonstrate understanding and to use them in a variety of contexts and genres. Consider including in the lists words related to critical thinking skills such as persuasion, interpret, infer, and multiple perspectives; literacy skills such as questioning, connecting, predicting, and summarizing; and comprehension of abstract concepts such as equity, indices, ratios, and contour lines. Expanding academic vocabulary will help students read for meaning and work to support quality work.

Although each member of the senior team participated in at least one of the reviews, Clay cautions these conclusions are still preliminary; however, some interesting trends emerge. The consensus is that the three reviews are a sample only and more reviews in Lone Birch's schools are required to substantiate or challenge these initial findings. There is a need to continue with the process.

Thinking Out

Although there are specifics found in terms of commonalities, in fact they do not only apply to these three schools. These might be similar issues to note in your school or schools. To make sense of and learn from the reports, layer the findings and relate them back to your system's or school's directions. These are part of broader issues which, once identified, need to be addressed. Then, when looking at research and effective practices within your capacity to implement, be very specific.

A FOLLOW-UP PLAN

Once the patterns and trends across the reports are identified and the district or school is prepared to move forward, there is next a need to develop a work plan for operationalizing improvement. This is one way the organization learns. The plans have to include time lines, resources, roles, and responsibilities and be monitored if change is to become systemic and sustained. Consider a cycle back to relook at the schools that are reviewed early in the cycle to monitor improvements.

Using the Findings in a Learning Organization to Secure Accountability

Lea and the senior leadership team decide to create a small subcommittee, led by Clay, to sort out the effective drivers of change at Lone Birch from the ineffective ones. Looking over the three reports, there is concern that there may be too many recommendations. Perhaps they need to be more focused in their suggestions for improvement. The suggestions were guided by research, linked to the district's direction, and based on the individual school's evidence summary. The collaborative school review process, they hope, will limit fragmentation and PDD (pulled in different directions) and not increase it. The subcommittee will thus use the three reports as a catalyst to reexamine structures, resources, practices, and professional learning to inform school- and system-level improvement planning. They will review the suggestions to monitor the numbers and focus on the top three or four.

They will look for ways to diminish the persistence of variation in practice within schools and across schools. Lea perceives that the continued privatized practice and isolation teachers feel in some schools contributes to the wide variability in practice. As much as LBSD emphasized capacity building, it is still not enough. There needs to be reconsideration of the way professional learning is delivered centrally and in schools to build collective capacity. Lone Birch will use the subcommittee reports to explore ways to build capacity to create more coherent and collaborative cultures. As more reviews are completed their findings will influence the work of this subcommittee and the process will remain formative. They will begin to build a bank of "lessons learned." The committee will recommend revising the current Lone Birch District Improvement Plan (LBDIP) as follows:

- Limit the focus to a few impactful goals and tease out the key strategies from the many suggestions for improvement that will best assist Lone Birch to move forward on its improvement agenda.
- Create action plans at a school and system level to break down the strategies into manageable parts.
- Continue to monitor alignment and integration between the system and schools.
- Continue using data to identify trends and patterns to influence decision making and practices.
- Review the data gathered through the management system and explore ways to make the data more accessible and user-friendly to administrators and teachers.
- Build better ways to support collaboration among and between schools.

- Identify revisions required to the current collaborative school review process.
- Clarify the role of school supervisors for monitoring the progress of collaborative school reviews and implementing suggested changes.
- Establish a process for monitoring and reviewing within a continuous planning cycle.

Lea favors a three-year cycle for all schools but says she can live with a five-year cycle. Rather than have schools volunteer as they did for the pilot, the school supervisors agree that each of them will select the next schools for review from the volunteer list but also pick schools that had not volunteered. These will include both elementary and secondary schools. Senior administration will create a multiyear timetable so that the schools will know when their review is scheduled. Schools will be allowed to change their date with another school in their family, if a crisis arises that makes their collaborative school review not possible. This will form part of the formal report to the board members so they will be informed about the collaborative school reviews. Because there are resource costs associated with the collaborative school reviews, the senior team will put forward some options for the board members' consideration.

Monitoring and Evaluating
the Collaborative School Review Process

There is also discussion on how Lone Birch schools will be monitored after their first collaborative school review: How will the system know whether suggestions for improvement are making a difference? What should that process look like? The team develops a template to monitor the schools' progress; any school can use this tool to self-assess their degree along an implementation continuum (see Figure 6.4).

Another decision is to have a middle step before the second cycle of school reviews. This step entails creating panel-alike teams of administrators who can, within a year after the initial review, visit the partner school where the administration will share the report and the school improvement plan. They will then walk the school to demonstrate evidence of change.

Lea sees the development of supervisory skills as a key capacity-building opportunity for Lone Birch. She asks the supervisors to document their experiences from the three pilots. She has heard of the work of Lisa Millar, an experienced superintendent of schools for Pickering, Ontario for the Durham District School Board. Lisa's family of schools has consistently demonstrated improved student results. She intentionally plans with the school leadership teams; they monitor the evidence and learn from it to revise, modify, and focus improvement. Lea decides to use Lisa's experience to document the role of the superintendents as a model for Lone Birch to go forward. Lisa's description of the superintendent's role within the collaborative school review process, in terms of her family of schools for the Durham District School Board in Pickering, Ontario, Canada, is on the website and offers a detailed account, from a supervisor's lens, on how to strategically implement change. The templates she provides to Lea are shown in Figures 6.5 and 6.6.

Figure 6.4	School Self-Review Tool						
School Self-Review							
School				Date			
School Team Members				B = Beginning Implementation, D = Developing Implementation, I = Implementation, S = Sustainability (coherent, intentional, and ongoing practice)			
Focus Component of SIP	**Evidence School, Classroom, Student**	**B**	**D**	**I**	**S**	**Status and Next Steps**	
Literacy	*School*						
	• Data collected and analyzed to identify strengths, areas of concern, and gaps						
	• Summary of SIP strategic direction						
	• Effective schoolwide literacy interventions and high-yield strategies						
	• Opportunities for 21st-century learning						
	• Capacity building with professional practice, professional learning, and inquiry						
	• Structures to support the needs of diverse learners						
	Classroom						
	• Comprehensive literacy program						
	• Clear connections between reading, writing, oral communication, and media literacy						
	• Teaching process supporting student learning in practicing, applying, and seeing connections and relevance						

(Continued)

Figure 6.4 (Continued)

School Self-Review

School		Date					
School Team Members		B = Beginning Implementation, D = Developing Implementation, I = Implementation, S = Sustainability (coherent, intentional, and ongoing practice)					
Focus Component of SIP	Evidence School, Classroom, Student	B	D	I	S	Status and Next Steps	
	• Evidence of learning—learning goals, anchor charts, academic vocabulary, success criteria, and other cuing systems • Coconstructed learning • Questions and tasks are rich and purposeful, with a focus on higher-order thinking • Descriptive feedback used regularly to inform improvement • Scaffolded learning *Students* • Know what and why they are learning • Know what good work looks like • Can explain their strengths and next steps • Acquire, develop, and refine their skills in reading, writing, oral communication, and media literacy • Listen actively, question for different purposes, and contribute to group learning						

	• Retell, summarize, analyze, synthesize, and reflect on a variety of texts to build meaning • Use critical literacy and numeracy skills to think about texts they experience (context, problems) and texts they create (interpret, model, create)
Numeracy	*School* • Data collected and analyzed to identify strengths, areas of concern, and gaps • Summary of SIP strategic direction • Effective schoolwide numeracy interventions and high-yield strategies • Opportunities for 21st-century learning • Capacity building with professional practice, professional learning, and inquiry • Structures to support the needs of diverse learners *Classroom* • Comprehensive numeracy program • Modelling and encouragement • Three-part lessons, Bansho-designed for students to problem solve, make connections, and share and communicate their thinking mathematically • Evidence of learning—learning goals, anchor charts, academic vocabulary, success criteria, and other cuing systems • Coconstructed learning involving problem solving that integrates across strands and rich authentic tasks to promote conceptual understanding

(Continued)

Figure 6.4   (Continued)

School Self-Review

School							
			Date				
School Team Members			B = Beginning Implementation, D = Developing Implementation, I = Implementation, S = Sustainability (coherent, intentional, and ongoing practice)				
Focus Component of SIP	**Evidence School, Classroom, Student**	**B**	**D**	**I**	**S**	**Status and Next Steps**	
	• Descriptive feedback to inform improvement • Scaffolded learning *Students* • Know what and why they are learning in terms of mathematical approaches, ideas, and communication • Know what good work looks like • Can explain their strengths and next steps • Use critical literacy and numeracy skills to think about texts they experience (context, problems) and texts they create (interpret, model, create) • Participate in peer moderation experiences						
School community, culture, and caring	*School* • Staff involved in improvement planning • Structures to prioritize teaching/learning time— uninterrupted blocks, scheduling, in-school meetings						

- Remedial Interventions—nutrition programs, tutoring programs
- Safe and secure plans and promotional strategies—future aces, character education, citizenship, eco-schools
- Schoolwide progressive discipline developed, communicated, and supported
- Use of restorative practices
- Meaningful role of school council in assisting staff to support teaching and learning and working with parents on communication and on improvement planning at the school
- Engagement of parents/guardians as partners
- Communication to parents/guardians in appropriate languages—web, newsletters
- Engagement of the community and elders (where appropriate) to enhance learning opportunities for students
- Opportunities and structures to support productive parent-teacher-student interactions

Classroom

- Parents and community serving as role models
- Mutually developed classroom norms communicated and supported
- Accommodations and modifications regarding progressive discipline
- Show the value of links from school to home
- Ongoing and clear communication to parents/guardians in appropriate languages

(Continued)

Figure 6.4 (Continued)

School Self-Review

School		Date				
School Team Members		B = Beginning Implementation, <u>D</u> = Developing Implementation, <u>I</u> = Implementation, <u>S</u> = Sustainability (coherent, intentional, and ongoing practice)				
Focus Component of SIP	Evidence School, Classroom, Student	B	D	I	S	Status and Next Steps
	Students • Understand the values and key messages • Know what the classroom norms are and why they are important • Can describe active listening and participating • Can explain their strengths and next steps					
Programs and Pathways	*School* • Programs and pathways addressing all destinations and reflecting the diversity, needs, and interests of the school's population • Provision for career opportunities linked to all pathways • A variety of diverse programs to meet the needs of all learners accessible • Students supported through learning profiles, career planning, and annual learning goals					

- Students provided with out of school experiences and activities linked to in-school learning
- Processes and structures to support transitions

Classroom

- Inclusive teaching reflecting individual needs and preferences
- Instruction supporting students' informed choices
- Respect for and opportunities to learn about all destinations
- Authentic learning experiences and experiential learning opportunities provided
- Opportunities and structures for students to acquire, practice, and demonstrate citizenship skills
- Diverse needs and interests addressed in the teaching and learning process
- Students' voice encouraged and respected

Students

- Participate in accountable talk
- Can articulate their needs and interests
- Understand (with their parents) the range of options in terms of programs and pathways
- Participate in out of school experiences and activities linked to in-school learning
- Participate in programs that develop leadership, teamwork, and advocacy
- Demonstrate action-orientated global mindedness
- Reflect on their learning

181

Figure 6.5	Monitoring Tool for Elementary Principals	

1. Teachers have deconstructed curriculum expectations.

	No	Early Adoption/ Initial Implementation	Implementation in Process	Embedded Practice
Primary				
Junior				
Intermediate				

2. On my walkthroughs, students can describe what they are learning, why they are learning it, and what to do if they do not understand it.

	No	Early Adoption/ Initial Implementation	Implementation in Process	Embedded Practice
Primary				
Junior				
Intermediate				

3. The teachers and students participate in the development of learning goals.

	No	Early Adoption/ Initial Implementation	Implementation in Process	Embedded Practice
Primary				
Junior				
Intermediate				

4. The teachers and students coconstruct success criteria.

	No	Early Adoption/ Initial Implementation	Implementation in Process	Embedded Practice
Primary				
Junior				
Intermediate				

5. The teachers have developed and use anchor/criteria charts, rubrics, or exemplars to help students understand what quality work looks like and to identify next steps in their learning.

	No	Early Adoption/ Initial Implementation	Implementation in Process	Embedded Practice
Primary				
Junior				
Intermediate				

6. The teachers ensure students have the opportunity to evaluate their own work using specific tools and exemplars.				
	No	Early Adoption/ Initial Implementation	Implementation in Process	Embedded Practice
Primary				
Junior				
Intermediate				

7. Teachers work with their colleagues to deconstruct curriculum expectations.				
	No	Early Adoption/ Initial Implementation	Implementation in Process	Embedded Practice
Primary				
Junior				
Intermediate				

8. Teachers moderate over student work.				
	No	Early Adoption/ Initial Implementation	Implementation in Process	Embedded Practice
Primary				
Junior				
Intermediate				

Next Steps				
Area of Focus	Strategies	Action Plan	Time Lines	Evaluation

Figure 6.6	Monitoring Tool for Secondary Principals

1. Teachers have deconstructed curriculum expectations.

	No	Early Adoption/ Initial Implementation	Implementation in Process	Embedded Practice
English				
Mathematics				

2. On my walkthroughs, students can describe what they are learning, why they are learning it, and what to do if they do not understand it.

	No	Early Adoption/ Initial Implementation	Implementation in Process	Embedded Practice
English				
Mathematics				

3. The teachers and students participate in the development of learning goals.

	No	Early Adoption/ Initial Implementation	Implementation in Process	Embedded Practice
English				
Mathematics				

4. The teachers and students coconstruct success criteria.

	No	Early Adoption/ Initial Implementation	Implementation in Process	Embedded Practice
English				
Mathematics				

5. The teachers have developed and use anchor/criteria charts, rubrics, or exemplars to help students understand what quality work looks like and to identify next steps in their learning.

	No	Early Adoption/ Initial Implementation	Implementation in Process	Embedded Practice
English				
Mathematics				

6. The teachers ensure students have the opportunity to evaluate their own work using specific tools and exemplars.

	No	Early Adoption/ Initial Implementation	Implementation in Process	Embedded Practice
English				
Mathematics				

7. Teachers work with their colleagues to deconstruct curriculum expectations.

	No	Early Adoption/ Initial Implementation	Implementation in Process	Embedded Practice
English				
Mathematics				

8. Teachers moderate over student work.

	No	Early Adoption/ Initial Implementation	Implementation in Process	Embedded Practice
English				
Mathematics				

9. Teachers provide feedback to students that is timely, explicit, constructive, and linked to success criteria to improve their learning.

	No	Early Adoption/ Initial Implementation	Implementation in Process	Embedded Practice
English				
Mathematics				

10. Teachers provide targeted intervention strategies that assist students to be successful.

	No	Early Adoption/ Initial Implementation	Implementation in Process	Embedded Practice
English				
Mathematics				

(Continued)

Figure 6.6   (Continued)

11. Teachers provide written descriptive feedback based on success criteria.

	No	Early Adoption/ Initial Implementation	Implementation in Process	Embedded Practice
English				
Mathematics				

12. Teachers use differentiated instruction.

	No	Early Adoption/ Initial Implementation	Implementation in Process	Embedded Practice
English				
Mathematics				

13. Teachers use direct instruction.

	No	Early Adoption/ Initial Implementation	Implementation in Process	Embedded Practice
English				
Mathematics				

14. Teachers use guided practice and review.

	No	Early Adoption/ Initial Implementation	Implementation in Process	Embedded Practice
English				
Mathematics				

15. Teachers use small-group instruction to target a skill.

	No	Early Adoption/ Initial Implementation	Implementation in Process	Embedded Practice
English				
Mathematics				

16. Teachers use monitoring and reassessment.

	No	Early Adoption/ Initial Implementation	Implementation in Process	Embedded Practice
English				
Mathematics				

17. Teachers use extra support/reteaching.				
	No	Early Adoption/ Initial Implementation	Implementation in Process	Embedded Practice
English				
Mathematics				

18. Teachers use special education resource teachers (SERT) support.				
	No	Early Adoption/ Initial Implementation	Implementation in Process	Embedded Practice
English				
Mathematics				

Next Steps				
Area of Focus	Strategies	Action Plan	Time Line	Evaluation

IN SUMMARY

This chapter has focused on layering an accountability structure on the collaborative school review process to assess the level of impact on student achievement. We cannot stress enough that the actual reviews are not the end, but part of a continuous improvement approach. Unpacking the reviews at the school and system level, cycling back to schools that have had reviews, and teasing out the systemic implications are critical aspects of the four-quadrant overlay that we have introduced. We suggest establishing components that are not usually associated with school reviews. These include articulating the accountability structure for the process, rigorously analyzing the findings and their implications for the school and the broader system, developing a plan of action to ensure that the suggestions for improvement are followed through, and monitoring and evaluating the collaborative school review process.

This new and rigorous focus on accountability is a powerful variable that turns the collaborative school review into a systemic change management strategy. Collaborative school reviews are not isolated efforts within a school, but rather they become the norm for a district with their systemic and consistent implementation. Findings and suggestions for improvement are carefully analyzed and opportunities for improvement rigorously implemented. The value of the process is vigilantly monitored and evaluated to ensure continuing relevance.

If you have developed the system we suggest throughout this resource, you now have a clearly articulated process for securing accountability for your collaborative school review process. This includes:

- Establishing the accountability structure with roles, responsibilities, reporting processes, and follow-up requirements
- A layered analysis within which to identify school-based issues and opportunities, but more important, those issues and opportunities that could dramatically change teaching practice across the system
- An action plan for implementing each of the suggested changes, ensuring that progress is rigorously and regularly monitored
- A process to monitor and evaluate the continuing value of the collaborative school review process to ensure relevance and continuing refinement of the policy, the model, process, and protocols

For further information and additional resources, please visit the website associated with this book at www.collaborativeschoolreviews.com.

7 Creating Excellence and Innovation From the Inside Out

As noted at the beginning, collaborative school reviews offer schools and school districts a valuable tool to improve from the inside out. They provide this within a structure that raises the level of accountability and ensures a more immediate and sustainable change management process. One of the paradoxes of improvement is that although research has provided findings that illuminate effective and results-based practices, we still maintain ineffective practices. Exhorting schools and school systems to be more effective and efficient without the direction, framework, and supports that allow for deep and sustained change means that improvement will continue to be, for the most part, disparate and superficial. Collaborative school reviews, grounded in the strategic change management framework we introduced, allow for the development of new skills and knowledge as well as a reexamination of processes and practices to lead to more intentional, coherent, and sustained change. This is especially true when school districts are being asked to implement complex change such as with the CCSS.

Underlying collaborative school reviews is a commitment for unrelenting implementation of high expectations for improved student achievement. The process is premised on a collaborative yet methodical approach to change that is focused and critical to improvement in student learning.

● 189

The Lone Birch case study reflects the differences between schools—the lack of consistency among and between classrooms and schools is a reality in most districts. The collaborative review process is designed to decrease variability and increase effectiveness. We acknowledge that sustained and deep change takes time and that there has to be a defined cycle with time lines to build the capacity; there also must be a strong commitment to see the change through. Unexpected pressures and issues will arise.

Collaborative school reviews build more than technical skills or management skills—they are embedded in strategic leadership. If attention is paid to the design and planning quadrants introduced, then intentionality, common understanding, shared support, and context can be embedded in the process. Protocols are determined and strategic communication established. Information is shared top-down and bottom-up. Targeted capacity building supports the process for the reviews and the external review teams. For the school and system staff, targeted capacity building ensures that the school improvement teams and teaching staff, the external review teams, and senior administration have the skills and knowledge to ensure the effectiveness of the reviews. These become shared skills and understandings that begin to change the very fiber of the organization's overall capacity. Implementation as a result is not reactive but proactive, and as Lea our Lone Birch superintendent maintained, at the end of the collaborative school review process, the system knows more about coherency, alignment, and impact than they did before. For your school and school system, you will know more than you know now. Collaborative school reviews, by following a defined process, create an environment and a structure supportive of change.

Creating areas for focus and feedback and gathering the supporting evidence are tasks designed to be collaborative, with staff cooperatively working together to select their priorities and evidence. It becomes part of the learning process. This too assists building shared understanding and commitment to the change process. Vision and action become complementary as capacity building and accountability occur simultaneously. When combined, these become drivers of deep systemic change. Implementation is structured. At this stage, capacity has been built and protocols should keep the focus on improving achievement. The onsite observations and conversations, again, contribute to a culture of learning and change. Collaborative school reviews provide a mechanism to assess alignment and coherency alongside the stated goals of the individual schools and the system. Feedback mirrors the findings to the school and school system. Written reports provide clear and descriptive feedback. Unpacking the results of the collaborative school reviews, both at a school and system level, forms part of an evidence-based approach to decision making. The results create a basis for dialogues on data.

The more the results are collectively unpacked and the process is shared, the more collaborative the focus is on improving student learning and staff learning. Our aim is whole-school conversations as opposed to decision making by a few. The process of collaborative school reviews can act as an antidote to privatized practice. Assessing the degree of coherency, intentionality, and alignment is only part of the process.

For change to become embedded, then actions must ensue from the results of collaborative school reviews. Sustained change must be based on the findings and data sets and guided by context and research. Communication of the results is integral. The process must be continuously monitored—remember what Lea says—what gets monitored gets done. In the accountability quadrant, revisions are suggested as a result of unpacking results and analysis. This unpacking and analysis informs the design and planning, and the cycle continues again.

We believe that the desire to raise the bar and close achievement gaps is real. The demands for improvement achievement from the public and governments provide urgency to the need for change. The expectation is for school and system administrators to be instructional leaders. School-based administrators are second only to teachers to impacting student achievement (Leithwood, Louise, Anderson, & Wahlstrom, 2004). District leadership is critical to creating an environment of accountability and capacity building in terms of instructional leadership. System leaders can create the vision. Structure, resources, and monitoring—together these can take the system from the theory of action to change. The support and expectations must be clear, visible, and widely understood.

As a sector, our legacy is fragmented superficial fixes. We want equity and equality. We want to maintain academic optimism and raise bars and close gaps—governments and the public want all of this yesterday—but the path to improvement is complex. We personally have experienced political demands for immediate change and plethora of program initiatives in governments and in districts. As we have explained, deep and sustained improvement doesn't result from superficialities. No one policy or program or training package will solve the complexity inherent in sustained educational change. Collaborative school reviews are not the answer, but part of the answer. By maintaining fidelity to the strategic framework, one that is core to their design and application, collaborative reviews can build common understanding, promote collegial dialogues, show schools and districts where they are along the continuum to improvement, and assist in finding paths to achieve aligned, intentional, and coherent change.

The process is contextually driven so it is not a question of adopting a predesigned and expensive program. It provides tools to help you conduct your day-to-day activities and discharge your leadership roles in new and more effective ways. What we suggest are changes to how you use your role and time. We aim to balance theory and practice, and make this resource practical to demonstrate how change can be doable using both inside out and outside in. To improve student learning, we must improve adult learning and change the focus of our activities. Schools and school systems must be learning systems. The adults in the system must be willing and able and their learning continuous. Collaborative school reviews focus on this ability to learn and your accountability for improving teaching and student achievement. Your more effective use of data about teaching and learning in your schools will ensure that clear evidence of progress and capacity building become a fact of life for your education system.

Education as a sector is often buffeted by immediate demands to implement new programs, new technologies, and new skills. Often these initiatives are disparate, and not aligned or impactful. Schools and school systems are flooded with solutions purported to fix education and in the end not much changes. As we demonstrate, a few measureable, aligned, and research-informed goals based on multiple data sources are preferential to "the flavor of the month." Sustained change requires hard and focused efforts across the whole system. We believe this requires a rethinking of roles, responsibilities, and how leadership time and staff resources are applied. A shift would have system and school leaders take greater responsibility for school reviews and thus ensure the linking of teaching strategies to student achievement data. Although this requires capacity building, in the end, this is less costly than the rash and disconnected efforts currently in play that aim for short-term gains.

Both of us wish you a productive and collaborative journey to improve and sustain gains in student achievement.

For further information and additional resources, please visit the website associated with this book at www.collaborativeschoolreviews.com.

References and Further Reading

Ackoff, R., & Addison, H. (2010). *Systems thinking for curious managers: With 40 new management flaws.* Axminster, Devon, UK: Triarchy Press.

Armstrong, A. (2011). Lesson study puts collaborative lens on student learning. *Tools for Schools, 14*(4), 1–3.

Barber, M., Moffit, B., & Kihn, P. (2010). *Deliverology 101: A field guide for educational leaders.* Thousand Oaks, CA: Corwin.

Bauer, S., & Brazer, D. (2012). *Using research to lead school improvement: Turning evidence into action.* Thousand Oaks, CA: Sage.

Bernhardt, V. (2004). *Data analysis for continuous improvement* (2nd ed.). Larchmmont, NY: Eye on Education.

Berry, B. (2011). *Teaching 2030: What we must do for our students and our public schools—now and in the future.* New York: Teachers College Press.

Blase, J., & Blase, J. (2006). The teacher's principal. *The Learning Principal, 1*(4), 1, 6, 7.

Burke, W., Lake, D., & Paine, J. (2009). *Organization change: A comprehensive reader.* San Francisco: Jossey-Bass.

Christensen, C., Horn, M., & Johnson, C. (2008). *Disrupting class: How innovation will change the way the world learns.* New York: McGraw-Hill.

Cialdini, R. B. (2001). Systematic opportunism: An approach to the study of tactical social influence. In J. P. Forgas & K. D. Williams (Eds.), *Social influence: Direct and indirect processes* (pp. 25–39). Philadelphia: Psychology Press.

City, E., Elmore, R., Fiarman, S., & Teitel, L. (2009). *Instructional rounds in education: A network approach to improving teaching and learning.* Cambridge, MA: Harvard Education University Press.

Costa, A., Garmston, R., & Zimmerman, D. (2012). Cognitive capital: An investment in teacher quality. *Education Week, 32*(12), 26, 32.

Curtis, G. (2011). *Education updates.* Alexandria, VA: Association for Supervision and curriculum Development.

Curtis, R. (2011). *Achievement first: Developing a teacher performance management system that recognizes excellence.* Washington, DC: Aspen Institute.

Curtis, R., & City, E. (2009). *Strategy in action.* Boston: Harvard University Press.

Darling-Hammond, L. (2010). *Evaluating teacher effectiveness.* Washington, DC: Center for American Progress.

Darling-Hammond, L. (2011, May). Lessons from the US. Speech. Australian Association for Research in Education Conference, The University of Sydney.

Dean, C., Hubbell, E., Pitler, H., & Stone, B. (2012). *Classroom instruction that works* (2nd ed.). Alexandria, VA: Association for Supervision and Curriculum Development.

Dufour, R., Dufour, R., Eaker, R., & Many, T. (2010). *Learning by doing: A handbook for professional learning communities at work* (2nd ed.). Bloomington, IN: Solution Tree Press.

Dufour, R., & Marzano, R. (2011). *Leaders of learning.* Bloomington, IN: Solution Tree Press.

Eck, J., Stringfield, S., Reynolds, D., Schaffer, E., & Bellamy, G. T. (2011). *Noteworthy perspectives: High reliability organizations in education.* Denver, CO: McREL.

Freedman, B. (2007). *Looking for leadership: Increasing principal presence through classroom-walk-throughs and the resulting influence on principal-teacher relationships* (Doctoral thesis). Toronto: OISE/University of Toronto.

Fullan, M. (2010). *Motion leadership: The skinny on becoming change savvy.* Thousand Oaks, CA: Corwin.

Fullan, M. (2011). *Choosing the wrong drivers for system reform.* Victoria, AU: Centre for Strategic Education. Retrieved from www.michaelfullan.ca/home_articles/SeminarPaper204.pdf

Furhman, S., & Elmore, R. (2004). *Redesigning accountability systems for education.* New York: Teachers College Press.

Grose, K., & Strachan, J. (2012). *Flash forward: Rethinking learning.* Seattle, WA: Lantern Press.

Hancock, L. (2001, September). Why are Finland's schools successful? *Smithsonian Magazine.* Retrieved from www.smithsonianmag.com/people-places/Why-Are-Finlands-Schools-Successful.html#ixzz1kJrxE2qc

Harris, A., Day, C., Hopkins, D., Hatfield, M., Hargreaves, A., & Chapman, C. (2003). *Effective leadership for school improvement.* New York: Routledge Press.

Harvard Educational Review. (2011). *Adolescent literacy.* Cambridge, MA: Harvard Educational Press.

Hattie, J. (2009). *Visible learning.* London: Routledge.

Hattie, J. (2012). *Visible learning for teachers: Maximizing impact on learning.* London: Routledge.

Hilliard, A. G., III. (1998). *SBA: The reawakening of the African mind.* Gainesville, FL: Makare Publishers.

Hirsh, S., & Hord, S. (2012). *A playbook for professional learning: Putting the standards into action.* Oxford, OH: Learning Forward.

Hord, S., & Sommers, W. (2008). *Leading professional learning communities: Voices from research and practice.* Thousand Oaks, CA: Corwin.

Kielburger, C., Kielburger, M., & Page, S. (2010). *The world needs your kid.* Toronto: Me to We Books.

Leithwood, K., Louis, K., Wahlstrom, K., Anderson, S., Mascall, B., & Michlin, M. (2009). *Learning from district efforts to improve student achievement.* New York: Wallace Foundation.

Leithwood, K., Louise, K. S., Anderson, S., & Wahlstrom, K. (2004). *How leadership influences student learning.* New York: The Wallace Foundation.

Levin, B. (2008). *How to change 5000 schools.* Cambridge, MA: Harvard Education Press.

Levin, B. (2010). Leadership for evidence-informed education. *School Leadership and Management, 30*(4), 303–315.

Levin, B. (2012). *More high school graduates.* Toronto: OPC and Thousand Oaks, CA: Corwin.

Little, J. (1990). The persistence of privacy: Autonomy and initiative in teachers' professional relations. *Teachers College Record, 91*(4), 509–536. Retrieved from www.tcrecord.org/Content.asp?ContentId=406

Lortie, D. (2002). *The schoolteacher: A sociological study* (2nd ed.) Chicago: University of Chicago Press.

Marzano, R. (2003). *What works in schools: Translating research into action.* Alexandria, VA: Association for Supervision and Curriculum Development.

Marzano, R., Frontier, T., & Livingston, D. (2011). *Effective supervision: Supporting the art and science of teaching.* Alexandria, VA: Association for Supervision and Curriculum Development.

Marzano, R., & Waters, T. (2009). *District leadership that works.* Bloomington, IN: Solution Tree Press.

Marzano, R., Waters, T., & McNulty, B. (2005). *School leadership that works.* Alexandria, VA: Association for Supervision and Curriculum Development.

Office for Standards in Education (OFSTED). (2012). *The framework for school inspection.* Retrieved from www.ofsted.gov.uk

Ontario Ministry of Education. (2010). *School effectiveness framework.* Toronto: Queen's Printer. Retrieved from http://resources.curriculum.org/secretariat/framework/index.shtml

Organisation for Economic Co-operation and Development (OECD). (2011). *Education at a glance.* Retrieved from www.oecd.org/education/education economyandsociety/educationataglance2011oecdindicators.htm

Pfeffer, J., & Sutton, R. (2000). *The knowing-doing gap: How smart companies turn knowledge into action.* Boston: Harvard Business School Press.

Phillips, V., & Hughes, R. (2012). Teacher collaboration: The essential ingredient. *Education Week, 32*(13), 32.

Pink, D. (2009). *Drive: The surprising truth about what motivates us.* New York: Riverhead Books.

Pinnell, G., & Fountas, I. (2011). *The continuum of literacy learning* (2nd ed.). Portsmouth, NH: Heinemann Press.

Portin, B., Knapps, M., Dareff, S., Feldman, S., Russell, F., Samuelson, C., & Yeh, T. (2009). *Leadership for learning improvement in urban schools,* Seattle: Center for the Study of Teaching and Policy, University of Washington.

Prensky, M. (2010). *Teaching digital natives: Partnering for real learning.* Thousand Oaks, CA: Corwin.

Programme for International Student Assessment (PISA). (2011). *PISA 2009 key findings.* Retrieved from www.oecd.org/pisa/pisaproducts/pisa2009keyfindings.htm

Reeves, D. (2005). *Accountability in action* (2nd ed.). Englewood, CO: Advanced Learning Press.

Sahlberg, P. (2011). *Finnish lessons: What can the world learn from educational change in Finland?* New York: Teachers College Press.

Schwartz, S., & Pollishuke, M. (2012). *Creating the dynamic classroom* (2nd ed). Toronto: Pearson Education Canada.

Sharratt, L., & Fullan, M. (2009). *Realization: The change imperative for deepening district-wide reform.* Toronto: OPC and Thousand Oaks, CA: Corwin.

Sharratt, L., & Fullan, M. (2012). *Putting faces on the data.* Toronto: OPC and Thousand Oaks, CA: Corwin.

Schwartz, & S. Pollishuke, M. (2012). *Creating the dynamic classroom* (2nd ed.). Toronto: Pearson Education Canada.

Sinek, S. (2009). *Start with why: How great leaders inspire everyone to take action.* New York: Portfolio Press.

Tapscott, D. (2009). *Grown up digital: How the net generation is changing your world.* New York: McGraw-Hill.

Tate, M. L. (2004). *"Sit and get" won't grow dendrites: 20 professional learning strategies that engage the adult brain.* Thousand Oaks, CA: Corwin.

Van Clay, M., Soldwedel, P., & Many, T. (2011). *Aligning school districts as PLCs.* Bloomington, IN: Solution Tree Press.

Wessling, S. (2011). Trust, professionalism, truth. *Education Update, 53*(5).

Index

Pages followed by f indicate figures. CSR stands for collaborative school reviews.

CORWIN

A SAGE Company

The Corwin logo—a raven striding across an open book—represents the union of courage and learning. Corwin is committed to improving education for all learners by publishing books and other professional development resources for those serving the field of PreK–12 education. By providing practical, hands-on materials, Corwin continues to carry out the promise of its motto: **"Helping Educators Do Their Work Better."**

The Ontario Principals' Council (OPC) is a voluntary association for principals and vice-principals in Ontario's public school system. We believe that exemplary leadership results in outstanding schools and improved student achievement. To this end, we foster quality leadership through world-class professional services and supports. As an ISO 9001 registered organization, we are committed to **"quality leadership—our principal product."**